This series offers the concerned reader basic guidelines
and *practical* applications of religion for today's world.
Although decidedly Christian in focus and emphasis,
the series embraces all denominations and modes of
Bible-based belief relevant to our lives today. All volumes
in the Steeple series are originals, freshly written to
provide a fresh perspective on current—and yet
timeless—human dilemmas. This is a series for our times.

Among the books in the series:

James W. Steele is a minister, teacher, youth worker, chaplain, and counselor. A firm believer that God's word is the answer, Dr. Steele has had extensive experience counseling with all ages and acquainting himself with life's problems. He has written articles in religious periodicals and magazines as well as columns for local newspapers. He holds a doctorate in ministry.

Bible Solutions to Problems of Daily Living

James W. Steele

A SPECTRUM BOOK

Prentice-Hall, Inc., Englewood Cliffs, New Jersey 07632

Library of Congress Cataloging in Publication Data

Steele, James W. (James William) (date)
    Bible solutions to problems of daily living.

    (Steeple books)
    (A Spectrum Book)
    Bibliography: p.
    1. Christian life.   2. Christian life—Biblical
teaching.   I. Title.   II. Series.
BV4501.2.S743   1983   248.4   83-3097
ISBN 0-13-078022-7
ISBN 0-13-078014-6 (pbk.)

1 2 3 4 5 6 7 8 9 10

ISBN 0-13-078022-7

ISBN 0-13-078014-6 (PBK.)

Editorial/production supervision by Peter Jordan
Cover design by Hal Siegel
Manufacturing buyer: Christine Johnston

Prentice-Hall International, Inc., *London*
Prentice-Hall of Australia Pty. Limited, *Sydney*
Prentice-Hall Canada Inc., *Toronto*
Prentice-Hall of India Private Limited, *New Delhi*
Prentice-Hall of Japan, Inc., *Tokyo*
Prentice-Hall of Southeast Asia Pte. Ltd., *Singapore*
Whitehall Books Limited, *Wellington, New Zealand*
Editora Prentice-Hall do Brasil Ltda., *Rio de Janeiro*

Contents

Preface

Is God really interested in the nitty-gritty things that plague us every day? Does He really care when we are in trouble? Does He really feel our pain when we are hurt or when we cry? If He does care, then He must have a special plan for our everyday living—including definite details for even the smallest facets of our lives. If He really does care, then He must want more than a mere existence for the human race. Since God made us and (by that fact) *owns* us, we should read and study His "Owner's Manual," the Holy Bible, and obey it in every detail in order to live life to the fullest.

In the beginning of the human race, God gave man very simple rules for living. The Lord said to Adam, "You are free to eat from any tree in the Garden; but you must not eat from the tree of the knowledge of good and evil, for when you eat of it you will surely die" (Gen. 2:16b-17). God was saying in essence, "You can live and be happy as long as you follow My rules, which include abstention from eating the fruit of one tree." As we know from history, mankind has since then been hungering for the forbidden fruit, or at least for a bite or two.

It is because Adam and Eve yielded to temptation that the Lord has handed down to us His "Owner's Manual," the Holy Bible. Contained in this "manual" are do's as well as don'ts for the human mechanism. Whether they are seen as positives or negatives, they should all be seen as basic rules of maintenance. They are for the smooth operation of the human being on a day-to-day basis. To ignore them means to suffer the consequences of a less-than-God-desired kind of existence. To embrace them is to live life at its best.

One can always think of someone who ignores the Bible truths for everyday living and who seemingly continues to enjoy a rich, full, prosperous life, whereas everything seems to go wrong in the life of the "saint" who daily endeavors to put God's rules into practice. I can point to some of the world's poorest who are some of the richest in God and some of the world's richest who are spiritually and morally impoverished.

While studying this unique "Owner's Manual" we need to understand that God intends what is best for us on an individual basis. Abraham Lincoln meant well when he reiterated the Constitution at Gettysburg saying, "All men are created equal." In God's sight we are equal, but we are born with different abilities and capabilities. We are not equal in physical abilities, emotional abilities, or mental abilities. The Word of God does not intimate that we are to be look-alikes, act-alikes, or think-alikes. God's rules for living fit every one of us equally well, although we are so unequal in so many ways. A size 42 suit would drape on a size 38 man, but it would burst at the seams when worn by a size 46 man. Likewise, God's "Owner's Manual," the Holy Bible, suits individuals—male and female—of all sizes, shapes, ages, colors, and languages.

Except where otherwise indicated, all bible references are taken from the New International Version.

chapter one

Why do
I need this?
I'm not sick!

The transmission in the car began to slip and cause an irritating situation. When I put the car in drive, I want it to drive. When it just sits there and quivers, I get a bit upset, especially since I didn't buy the car just to sit in it. I can sit in a chair and it's a lot cheaper. It was time for a trip to the car dealer. The mechanic asked, "When was the last time you had the transmission fluid changed and the bands adjusted?" My response showed my ignorance, "I didn't even know I was supposed to change the fluid. I have had the motor oil changed at regular intervals but that's all." "How many miles do you have on the car now?" asked the mechanic. "About 50,000 miles," I said sheepishly. I knew by now that the problem was not the fault of the manufacturer but that I should have better acquainted myself with the needs of the car. The mechanic, with apparent arrogance in his voice, added, "You should have had this thing in here 25,000 miles ago for maintenance—don't you have an owner's manual?" In reply, I just nodded. "Well, you might read it once in a while; the guy who designed this car knew what it would take to keep it running as it was intended to run."

If only I had opened the glove compartment, and gotten out the owner's manual and *read* it, I would have saved myself a lot of aggravation, time, and money. I thought of the expression, "When all else fails, read the directions." As I read the manual, I learned all about other services that should be completed if the vehicle was to give satisfactory service; things such as where the fuses are, what kind of bulbs are needed, how to get the most out of the accessories that cost so much, and how to take care of the vinyl top. I decided that the manufacturer knew more about the car than I did.

Many people have the idea that the Bible is merely a good book primarily for times and situations that we can't handle on our own. When we see that our lives have run amuck, then some may think it's time to get outside help, maybe even try God and His Word. In reality, many of life's problems can be averted by consulting the Bible on a regular basis; yes, even before problems develop.

God is our Maker, and He knows exactly what it takes for us to get the most out of life. He is interested in our having the best this life has to offer. We often settle for a life style far short of what He had in mind for us. What a pity and waste when people get on the wrong track and, rather than seek their Maker's help, continue in *their* own ways, making matters worse.

Once two men were traveling by car, and one fell asleep

to awaken later and discover they were on the wrong road going in the wrong direction. He said to his traveling companion, "Hey, man, we're on the wrong road; besides that, we're going in the wrong direction!" The driver of the car seemed calm and collected when he replied, "I've known that for an hour and a half." "Why didn't you turn around, then?" inquired the irritated passenger. The driver replied, "I was making such good time, I hated to stop!"

I've counseled many who, when asked if they had ever tried God's way, have sadly shaken their heads as if ashamed to say no. They came to see if I had a solution to their problems only as a last resort. That's like using God and His Word as a spare tire—there is no need for it until you have a flat.

There are some who know that the Word of God is the only true guide for living, but since its guidance is contrary to what they want (or think they want) in their life, they take a shortcut or a detour. Often shortcuts are dead-end roads, and detours are disastrous. The only sure way is *God's* way!

Before Jesus left to return to heaven, He said, "I am going there to prepare a place for you" (Jn. 14:2b). Multitudes today would say with Thomas, one of the twelve disciples, "Lord, we don't know where you are going, so how can we know the way?" (Jn. 14:5). Jesus' answer is as true now as it was then: "I am the way and the truth and the life" (Jn. 14:6). When Jesus says, "Follow me," He intends for us to follow His Word. Do what it says. It's like friends inviting you to come to their home and saying, "You won't find it by accident, so I'll leave you a map with directions. All you'll have to do is to follow the map; it will take you right to my house."

The Holy Bible does not merely *contain* God's Word, it *is* His Word! In support of His Word, God has given us this assurance, "All Scripture is God-breathed and is useful for teaching, rebuking, correcting and training in righteousness, so that the man of God may be thoroughly equipped for every good work" (2 Tim. 3:16-17). Friend, we are not really equipped for life apart from the Word of God! The Word of God is "useful for teaching." How we need to be taught! There are times when we need rebuking and correcting, and we always need "training in righteousness." God's purpose is not to put us in a straitjacket, but to equip us for life, here and hereafter.

I do not say that there will never be discouragements or trying times in the life of one who follows God and His Word, but as the apostle Paul said, "We are hard pressed on every side, but not crushed; perplexed, but not in despair; persecuted, but not abandoned; struck down, but not destroyed" (2 Cor. 4:8-9). The secret of it all is in the "but not's" of this Scripture! Every human being has had times of being hard pressed, of being perplexed, of being persecuted, and of being put down. But God's secret and that of the Bible is that we are not crushed, not without hope, not forsaken, and not destroyed. There's hope and help for the follower of the Bible!

The truth that eludes many people is that God intends for us to read and heed the Bible *before* trouble comes, before there is no other way. The adage, "An ounce of prevention is worth a pound of cure," is fitting here as nowhere else.

A long, long time ago God gave His people the Ten Commandments, found first in Exodus, chapter 20. The first three commandments had to do with man's relation to God— Don't have any other gods, don't make any idols of worship, and don't misuse the name of the Lord God. The next seven have to do with mankind's relationships one with another— rest on the Sabbath day, respect and revere your parents, don't murder, don't commit adultery, don't steal, don't lie, and don't long for that which belongs to another. When Jesus came, He said, "Do not think that I have come to abolish the Law or the Prophets; I have not come to abolish them but to fulfill them" (Mt. 5:17). Jesus came that we might have a meaningful relationship with the Father and a right relationship with our fellow citizens. He stressed that in order to get along with others we must *first* have a right relationship with God, our Maker.

The Bible is not just for the colossal, seemingly insurmountable problems that arise from time to time, it's for the *everyday* propositions as well. When I speak of everyday affairs of life, I don't mean to intimate that they are all trivial, for there are some everyday questions that demand an answer *now*; but I want you to know that your Maker is just as interested in your finding your misplaced car keys as He is in your decision to buy a new car. He is concerned about whatever is of concern to you! He was just as interested in the little boy who gave his lunch to feed the thousands as He was in the thousands (see Jn. 6:5-14). He was just as interested that the wedding feast in Cana went well as He was in raising His friend Lazarus of Bethany to new life (see Jn 2:11).

Don't ever say, "My problem is too small to bother Him," or "What does He care about my needs?" The same One who formed and fashioned the universe is the One who made the most delicate flower and put its faint, sweet perfume within. The One who flung the stars and planets into space is the same One who gave the honey bee the keen sense of direction to find that sweet nectar. The One who put the sun and moon in orbit is the same One who continues to orchestrate that silent, heavenly symphony; and that great Choreographer of the sky is keenly interested in you and me and our needs.

God only asks for a heart and mind yielded to Him and His will. In the Bible we learn that sometimes this goes against human nature, causing some to go on unyielded, thinking His price is too high. Jesus said, "If anyone would come after me, he must deny himself and take up his cross daily and follow me. For whoever wants to save his life will lose it, but whoever loses his life for me will save it" (Lk. 9:23-24). It does sound like a high price to pay until we consider the greater price to be paid for *not* yielding to Him. For instance, sometimes we shop for something we really want, but learn that the price is too high and settle for something less. However, as the days wear on we realize it would have been much better to have paid the price and have gotten the best. "The bitterness of poor quality lingers long after the sweetness of cheap price is forgotten." Whatever it costs you to have God's best— it's worth it!

The Bible is never out of date or out of step with our world. How ever the society may change, God's Word remains constant; we can always rely on it for every facet of our lives, at every age, in every situation; and if it's not good *for all*, it's not good *at all*.

There is a popular song called "I Did It My Way." It tells about all the accomplishments of a person's life, and then it is capped off with a smug phrase that indicates, "I always get my way and that's the best way." That may have been the sincere feeling of the lyricist, but my experience has proved that sometimes "my way" is not the best way; sometimes it is the worst way of all.

Today we are in about the same place spiritually as the Israelites were in the days of the Judges—"Everyone did as he saw fit" (Judg. 17:6). In the King James version this verse reads, "Every man did that which was right in his own eyes." I remember a saying I read while I was in high school, and I appreciate it more and more as the years go by: "A wise man knows how little he knows." I must be getting wiser if that saying is true, since I'm always realizing I know less and less about more and more! I don't know enough to run my life without God's guidance, and I doubt if you do either.

In Jesus' parable of the prodigal son, He tells how the young man spent all he had, did what he wanted to do, and really did it his way, but "when he came to his senses, he said, 'How many of my father's hired men have food to spare, and here I am starving to death! I will set out and go back to my father and say to him: Father, I have sinned against heaven and against you. I am no longer worthy to be called your son; make me like one of your hired men.' So he got up and went to his father" (Lk. 15:17-20). This parable is summed up in

9

the words, "When he came to his senses, . . . he got up and went to his father." He realized that that was the best place on earth for him to be.

If more husbands, wives, children, singles, young and old would come to their senses and come to God and His Word, many homes would be saved, lives would be spared heartache, and hurts would be healed.

Jesus said, "All that the Father gives me will come to me, and whoever comes to me I will never drive away" (Jn. 6:37). He simply means, "If you will come to me I will lead you—whoever you are, wherever you've been, and whatever you've done." He will take a young life and save it from the heartache that sin brings. He will take what's left of the old life and make the rest of it better than at first, or He will take shattered lives and broken dreams, pick up the pieces, and put them back together again. Talk about "super glue"! He can take homes that are breaking into tiny bits, pick up the fragments, and put them in order. He can take hopes that have been dashed on the rocks of anguish and make them something worthwhile. He can take aspirations that have been razed by the fires of sin and raise them to new life in Him. Oh yes, Jesus can do that and more if only you'll go to the Bible and follow it completely!

chapter two

"Jesus Loves the Little Children"

Jesus is interested in the family as a unit as well as individuals. God ordained the family, and Jesus, instructing the crowds that followed Him in Judea, gave some very pointed directives concerning divorce. Then, turning His attention to the little children who were brought to Him despite the rebuke of the disciples, He said, "Let the little children come to me, and do not hinder them, for the Kingdom of heaven belongs to such as these" (Mt. 19:14). These words made such an impact on the disciples that all three Synoptics record it (Mk. 10:13-16; Lk. 18:15-17) with Mark stating that He "put his hands on them and blessed them" (10:16b).

There can be no doubt that the love of God is not reserved just for those who are old enough to appreciate it. Children are sent as a blessing from the Lord. Psalm 127:3 states, "Sons are a heritage from the Lord, children a reward from him." Sometimes it may seem that you, as parent-recipient of these blessings and rewards, have been "overly blessed" and "excessively rewarded." I am speaking in terms of the behavior of children rather than their number.

When little Susie won't pick up her toys, do you feel like picking her up and "blessing" her, or do you feel that there is a "better remedy"? The answer is quite obvious. Correction, although difficult for the parent, is as necessary for the growth of a child as is a support tied to a young tree that is trying to grow in the wrong direction. When baby Billy has a tummy ache at 2 a.m. and the only answer is to take the little bundle in your arms and walk the floor, knowing that you have to be up at 6:30 and ready for a full day of work, does he seem like a reward, or does another word sum it up? The grind of walking a crying baby night after night is soon forgotten when he or she takes the first step or cuts the first tooth.

The long weeks and months of expectancy are not culminated in the birth of the infant, but rather in the maturation of that which is flesh of your flesh and blood of your blood. As that infant progresses through childhood, the teen years, and on into adulthood, the parents come to realize what God meant when He said children are rewards and blessings. I suppose there are few, if any, greater thrills for parents than to realize that this full-grown "child," born out of a mutual love between husband and wife, is now capable of making decisions, claiming a measure of independence, and going on with life. This should bring a great sense of fulfillment to the heart of the parent.

There is a tremendous amount of time, energy, prayer, love, and, yes, money that goes into bringing about this sense of fulfillment. Those who have no children are sometimes fearful that the love they have for each other will be diminished if a child should invade their cherished love nest. Nonetheless, God's plan for the home was that it might be complete with children. He said, "Be fruitful and increase in number; fill the earth and subdue it" (Gen. 1:28). Jesus, who loves little children, puts within us a capability to love those same little children. When Jesus said, "Seek first his kingdom and his righteousness, and all these things will be given to you as well" (Mt. 6:33), He meant, among other things, that our love would increase as our family increases. God intends that there be no conflict in our love. We must love Him first, then there will be enough to go around to the entire family. The mother or father who does not love his or her child is the mother or father who does not love God first. God wants us to have an altruistic love—that's love expanding. W. Robert Smith says, "Now the Lord gives children to parents not only that they may be provided for, but that they might be loved and disciplined. And they go together. Love without discipline is pure sentiment. Discipline without love is tyranny."[1]

"He who spares the rod hates his son, but he who loves him is careful to discipline him" (Prov. 13:24). Discipline will be discussed in another chapter, but note here the verse says, ". . . he who loves him is careful." Love is careful. Love is careful in every facet of life, and nowhere is it more important than when children are concerned. To be careful with our children is to be full of care. Be careful to teach those children of God and His love for them. God was speaking of the

---

[1] J. Allan Petersen, ed., *The Marriage Affair* (Wheaton, Ill.: Tyndale House Publishers, 1971), p. 127.

parents' responsibility to make His laws and ways known to their children when He said, "Teach them to your children, talking about them when you sit at home and when you walk along the road, when you lie down and when you get up" (Deut. 11:19).

Love that's full of care teaches children the ways of the Lord. While riding with one of my daughters in a pickup truck with an uncovered load in the back that should not get wet, I looked ahead and saw what was certain to be a downpour. There was no place to hide the cargo from the impending rain, and it seemed too late to turn around and go back. I said to my little firstgrader, "I hope that rain changes direction," and pointed to the blackened sky. In just a moment or two she said, "Daddy we won't get wet, I just prayed and asked Jesus to keep us dry." We didn't get wet, and I was relieved. But the fact that stayed in my mind was that this little child knew enough about God and had faith enough in her simple appeal to Him to believe He would answer. There was no question about it in her heart. Once Jesus "called a little child and had him stand among them. And He said: 'I tell you the truth, unless you change and become like little children, you will never enter the kingdom of heaven'" (Mt. 18:2-3). Do you suppose this simple, childlike faith was what Jesus was referring to?

Jesus loves little children because they're helpless. He loves them because they have no preconceived ideas about Him and no fear in trusting Him implicitly. He loves them because they have never knowingly sinned against Him—they are innocent.

Once I was a patient in a hospital primarily to have a

checkup. A physical therapist came to take me for some tests. Having come for me on several occasions, she knew that I was a minister. On the elevator she began to ask me some questions concerning God and the Church. Finally she asked a question that had long plagued her. She had become a mother only a couple of months before, and her infant had died within a matter of hours. "Did my baby go to heaven?" she asked. Her question might seem elementary to some, but to her it was haunting. I had never had any doubt or reason to ever ask this question. But now this young mother was distraught over this question to the point that it had caused a rift in her marriage. She was now separated from her husband over it. The unknown had so shaded her emotions that she was now nearing some real mental problems.

On that elevator and on into the physical therapy room, I assured her that her baby did indeed go to heaven and that although he could not come to her, she could some day go to him. I tried to satisfy her mind by explaining that it is sin that keeps one from heaven, and sin can be counted in a child's life only when he or she reaches the age at which God holds him or her accountable for actions. "Anyone, then who knows the good he ought to do and doesn't do it, sins" (Jas. 4:17). The "age of accountability" is different from child to child, but it is always when the child *voluntarily* disobeys God's directives. I never saw that young woman again, but I pray that she began to see the love and mercy of God and that Jesus loves little children.

Children need to learn the love of Jesus through their parents. They need to hear a warm "I love you" more often than most adults need to. A man once said, "My kids know I love them, look at all the things I buy them and the money I give them." But money and things cannot buy love, nor do they truly demonstrate affection. Certainly Jesus fed the children with the rest of the families when He took the loaves and fishes and multiplied them for the multitudes, but He also took time out of His extremely busy schedule to hold the children, bless them, and pray for them. There were adults to heal, instructions to give, miracles to perform, and a myriad of other tasks to complete in the short months of His earthly ministry, but Jesus loved little children and took time for them. We have recorded that He went out of His way to heal a demon-possessed child and to raise a dead girl to new life, and the list could go on and on concerning Jesus' love for children. A.F. Harper says, "To know that one is loved and cared for is to human personality what sunshine is to the growth of a flower. Children need this knowledge."[2]

The Bible assures children that they are loved and cared for by God, but there must be a loving and caring that can come only from the home situation. Little hurts to parents are big hurts to little children. Children can develop emotional problems of which the parents are not aware, and if the problems go unchecked, they can have a debilitating effect later in life. There are some signs a parent can recognize as an indication of the beginning of a problem. An unusual change in a child's eating habits or sleep pattern is often an indication. A reluctance to play and be active can be a sign of a physical or emotional disorder. A sudden change in school grades or a note from a teacher that something is not as it should be can

[2] A.F. Harper, *The Story of Ourselves* (Kansas City, Mo.: Beacon Hill Press, 1962), p. 153.

also be warning signs. When a problem is suspected, the parents should immediately take steps to correct it.

When our oldest daughter, Starletta, started her first year in college, my wife and I; our seventeen-year-old daughter; and our youngest daughter, Dawn, who was beginning first grade, went 300 miles to help Starletta get settled. We stayed the night, and late the next day we said our "goodbyes" with hugs and kisses and tearfully left the new freshman standing in front of that gigantic dormitory. I knew how I felt—it was terrible. Through my tears I looked at my wife beside me and knew that she was feeling the same pain—her tears told me. I drove on, barely seeing the road for the tears. Dawn was on her knees on the back seat looking out the back window trying to see her sister standing in front of the dormitory. Several blocks from the college, Dawn broke the silence with sobs that sounded like her heart would break. The tears flowed, and the emotions of that little girl were almost uncontrollable as she would catch her breath in audibly spasmodic contractions, almost gasping for breath. Finally we were able to quiet her enough to ask why she was crying so hard. She blurted out, "I won't see Starry anymore!" (Starry is Starletta's nickname.) We brought Dawn to the front seat, and her mother and I tried—and thought we succeeded—to convince her that Starry would be back home for a visit in a few weeks. All this took place over a distance of several miles. Although we were still sad, we finally all stopped crying.

Dawn went back to school the next day, and things seemed to be back to near normal—(as normal as it can be when one member of the family is missing, even if it is only off to college). A week later we received a note from Dawn's first-grade teacher asking if we would come to the school for a conference. At the conference, the teacher asked, "Has someone in Dawn's family—or maybe a friend—recently died?" She went on to say that Dawn's grades were going down and she seemed to have little interest in school. When the teacher would try to talk to her about her apparent unhappiness and disinterest in school, Dawn would always say, "I won't see Starry anymore!" The teacher thought Starletta must have died, or at least it seemed that way to Dawn. We finally got the situation straightened out, although we thought we had it straightened out just after we had left the college.

Sometimes parents can sense a deep need in a child; that's the best time to get to the bottom of the problem. The rest of the family knew that Starletta's going to college meant the children were growing up and that the separation would not be permanent, but the six-year-old only knew what her eyes saw and what her little heart felt, and neither one of them was good.

I believe that Jesus must have sensed troubled little hearts and took time to calm their fears. I believe He took time to stop and play with them on their turf, not just in the Temple. To follow His example, we too must take time to play their games, show interest in their interests, and cry with them when they cry. Too often parents have little or no time for their children. The old expression "Children are to be seen and not heard" is the motto of too many parents. True, there is a time when children should be seen and not heard, but little children can and should have a voice in this, their world, too.

When I was a child, my dad had to work most of the

time just to keep food on the table, a roof over our heads, and clothes on our backs, but I cherish the times we spent together as a family. We had planned times of togetherness when we played games that I'm sure must have seemed silly to my parents but meant much to us. Every year we took a vacation together. There was very little money to spend, and I still don't know how my parents managed the time and resources it took, but I still remember the good times we had together. The picnics will be remembered long after the aggravation of the ants is forgotten. Parents, don't "farm" the children out to stay with someone else while you go on vacation. Even if the vacation has to be shortened to fit the money available, give the children some good memories to carry over into their own families.

Little children should be brought to church by the parents. Don't ever let them get the idea that going to church is just for children and that parents don't need to attend. Having been a prison chaplain, I have talked with many men who said their parents *sent* them to Sunday school and church but the parents never went themselves. As soon as they got old enough, they felt too grown up to attend. The parents had used the church as a baby-sitting facility, and when the children realized what was happening, they wanted no part of it. Many of these men conceded that if their parents had been a part of the church too, their lives would probably have been different.

Most people in Jesus' day thought of children as mere appendages to be tolerated rather than enjoyed—to be *told* rather than *taught*. Jesus said that adults must be humble like children, teachable like children, trusting like children, de-

21

pendent like children, and loving like children. "And he said, I tell you the truth, unless you change and become like little children, you will never enter the kingdom of heaven. Therefore, whoever humbles himself like this child is the greatest in the kingdom of heaven. And whoever welcomes a little child like this in my name welcomes me" (Mt. 18:3-5). We so often picture children coming to Jesus that there must have been a genuine attraction to Him. His love for them must have shone through: Children do know if you really love them and they're attracted to that love. Take time to love children—Jesus did.

When a child is instructed either by word or action, a life is being molded. Sometimes children hear, "Your actions speak so loud I can't hear what you're saying." The same is true for adults. As we help mold young lives, do we live up to our own teaching? Do we say, in essence, "Do as I say and not as I do"? Children learn more from what they experience than from what they hear or read about. When they are young they are pliable, but in later years they are "set" in their ways. The author of the following is uncertain, but the message is clear:

> *I took a piece of plastic clay*
> *And idly fashioned it one day,*
> *And as my fingers pressed it still,*
> *It moved and yielded to my will.*

> *I came again when days were passed;*
> *The bit of clay was hard at last,*
> *The form I gave it still it bore,*
> *But I could change that form no more.*

I took a piece of living clay
And touched it gently day by day,
And molded with my power and art
A young child's soft and yielding heart.

I came again when years were gone;
It was a mind I looked upon;
That early impress still he wore,
And I could change that form no more.[3]

"We ought to encourage our children, bless them, provide for them, discipline them, instruct them, and set before them a Christ-like example. A Christ-like example is the greatest educational influence in the lives of our children."[4]

Parents should be as quick to verbalize their love for their children and to praise and encourage them for their achievements as they are to show their displeasure at their failures, as quick to caress and comfort as they are to put down and punish. The Bible says, "My dear brothers, take note of this: Everyone should be quick to listen, slow to speak and slow to become angry" (Jas. 1:19). Some parents are quick to listen to everyone *except* their own children. When correction is necessary, the child should have the opportunity to at least explain his or her side of the matter.

A father was once told by someone that his son had done something that he should not have done. The accusation was followed by the question, "What are you going to do

[3]Walter B. Knight, *Knight's Master Book of New Illustrations* (Grand Rapids, Mich.: William B. Eerdmans Publishing Company, 1956), p. 55.
[4]W. Robert Smith in *The Marriage Affair,* ed. Petersen.

about it?" The father, without asking his son about his role in the episode, came up from behind him and landed the palm of his hand with a whack on the back of the unsuspecting young head. That's not correction, but rather unjust punishment to satisfy the ego of a misguided father.

Just as children are different, so is the form of correction to be administered different from child to child—but it should always be fair and just! Since children are different by natural personality as well as physical characteristics (these are both God-given), our task is not to change those things that God has built into them, but rather to mold and fashion them tenderly to help them achieve the Master's will for their lives.

It is only natural for a person to think of his or her own needs but Jesus intends for us to have a balance in our love, one that will broaden excessively self-centered attachment and will make it affection for others as well. He said, "Love your neighbor as yourself" (Mt. 22:39). If we can be successful in teaching children to love the Lord above all and their neighbors as themselves, we have appropriately applied the Bible's teachings to those little children, whom Jesus loves.

chapter three

Too old for His love?

When do we outgrow the need for the love and care of our Creator? When does the time come when God is not so keenly interested in us and our cares and when He leaves us pretty much on our own?

The cry of thousands who have seen many years come and go is the same as that of the Psalmist: "Do not cast me away when I am old; do not forsake me when my strength is gone" (Ps. 71:9). "Even when I am old and gray, do not forsake me, O God" (71:18). These verses show that we never outgrow our need for God's love and concern. We never get so old that we no longer need outside help—help from our God.

A saintly woman over eighty years of age once called me to come to her home. Something was troubling her, and she wanted her pastor to pray with her. This dear woman had been sick and in the hospital for a prolonged stay. Her body was crippled, her eyes dimmed, and her voice weak, but her senses were keen and her heart was still sensitive to the whispers of her Lord. She began by saying, "Pastor, it seems that the devil is trying me more in these last days than he ever did before." This took me by surprise. I thought she "had it made" and that it was just a matter of her coasting right into heaven. Hadn't she lived with Jesus as the Lord of her life for the better part of sixty years? Were there still tests and trials?

She continued, "Satan is trying to get me to doubt by telling me that all these years I've lived for the Lord were for nothing." I learned right there that the devil does not give up as long as there is breath and consciousness. The tests had only changed from one variety to another, but the trials this dear child of God was having were every bit as real as any you or I have had or will have.

We prayed and read the Word of God, and she felt reassured that she was still God's and He was still hers. One of the Scriptures we read was Isaiah 46:4: "Even to your old age and gray hairs I am he, I am he who will sustain you. I have made you and I will carry you; I will sustain you and I will rescue you."

When God says He will not forsake us, He means that He'll be with us all the way to heaven! When He says He will sustain you, He means that there is no time in your life, even in old age, that He will not carry you over it! When He promises He will rescue you, He means that when it seems that Satan has the upper hand, He is right there and will snatch you up just in time!

When I travel the pathway so rugged and steep,
When I pass through the valley so dark and so deep,
And when snares for my soul by my foes have been set,
Jesus never has failed me yet.

Then I'll dread not the future, and fear not the foe.
I am safe in His keeping wherever I go;
For no soul that has trusted Him will He forget,
For He never has failed me yet.

W.J. Henry

Because of what God *has* done for you, you can expect Him to *continue* to do, because "Jesus Christ is the same yesterday and today and forever" (Heb. 13:8).

When we as Christians go through severe tests and trials, we should reflect on the tests and trials God has already seen us through. When we have hard places in our lives and wonder why, listen to the Bible's advice: "Consider it pure joy, my brothers, whenever you face trials of many kinds, because you know that the testing of your faith develops perseverance. Perseverance must finish its work so that you may be mature and complete, not lacking anything" (Jas. 1:2-4).

That's pretty strong for James to say, to consider all kinds of trials as pure joy; but the joy is not in the midst of the trial, it's for future reference. It's so that we may continue to press on and press on and on and on until we are "mature and complete, not lacking anything."

Titus says, "Teach the older men to be temperate, worthy of respect, self-controlled, and sound in faith, in love and in endurance" (2:2). He admonishes the Christian to be sound in the faith, to act worthy of the respect of others, to be steady and patient, and to act with loving kindness. If you can grow old with these attributes, you not only find living easier but you are also easier to live with. I've often said and haven't changed my mind, "Lord, let me grow old sweet and kind or not grow old at all."

I can recall some of the older men in the church where I grew up. At least a couple of them stand out in my mind as being all those things mentioned by Titus. I can almost feel the weight of their arm around my shoulders as a teenager as they would say, "How's it going Jim?" "I'm praying for you," or "Keep your hand in His, He has something good in store for you." I could feel their prayers as I was faced with the everyday pressures of being young. I still say, "Lord, let me be that kind of an old man." Those men were helps, not hindrances; they helped, not hurt; they prayed, not provoked. Those men acted worthy of the respect of others. I'm glad they were there when I needed an encouraging word and moral support.

Titus also says, "Likewise, teach the older women to be reverent in the way they live, not to be slanderers or addicted to much wine, but to teach the younger women" (2:3-4). "Likewise" means the older women are to behave in the same manner as the older men. They are to live lives above reproach and to be good teachers. Their primary task is to teach the younger women concerning those things that make for a good marriage and a happy home.

In verse 3, another translation puts it this way: "Older

women . . . do not be malicious gossips" (NASB). Older women and men, *don't be gossips!* Too often there is so little to do that the telephone becomes a tool of Satan, and too much time is spent "discussing" the affairs of others. Do you know that it doesn't have to be a lie to be gossip? The truth can be told when it would be better left untold; this becomes gossip. "I tell you that men [and women] will have to give account on the day of judgment for every careless word they have spoken" (Mt. 12:36).

Paul instructed young Timothy concerning younger widows, but his admonishment still applies to older men and women as well. He said, "They get into the habit of being idle and going about from house to house. And not only do they become idlers, but also gossips and busybodies, saying things they ought not to" (1 Tim. 5:13).

God has promised to take care of us in our old age, but there are some things He still expects of us. No, we never outgrow His care; His care for us and in all that we do. The Bible says, "In all things we are more than conquerors through him who loved us" (Rom. 8:37). This means that even in old age we are more than conquerors!

We never outgrow the need to clothe ourselves "with compassion, kindness, humility, gentleness and patience. Bear with each other and forgive whatever grievances you may have against one another. Forgive as the Lord forgave you. And over all these virtues put on love, which binds them all together in perfect unity" (Col. 3:12-14).

It is easy for some older ones to look at the younger ones and say, "We never did that when we were young" and to criticize the youth for being young and for doing what young people do. I'm not talking about condoning sin, but I do believe that if, when you are old, you want to be loved and respected by the young, you must be lovable and respectable toward them. Have you noticed that there are some older saints in the church that the young people like to be around and others who get the opposite reaction? Be lovable and you are more apt to be loved!

God will help you if you will obey the Bible, which says, "whatever is true, whatever is noble, whatever is right, whatever is pure, whatever is lovely, whatever is admirable—if anything is excellent or praiseworthy—think about such things" (Phil. 4:8).

Since I have never experienced old age with its unique complications and I may *never* face them, I can only draw on those who have had the experience. The one who penned Psalm 37 wrote, "I was young and now I am old, yet I have never seen the righteous forsaken or their children begging bread" (v. 23). These words issue from an experienced heart—experienced in the ways of the Lord.

The Lord is always good to His children, whether they are young children or old children. He only asks that you "Cast all your anxiety on him, *because he cares for you*" (1 Pet. 5:7).

chapter four

But you don't Know my husband!

"God saw all that he had made, and *it was very good*" (Gen. 1:31). But when He looked at lonely Adam, He said, "It is not good for the man to be alone" (Gen. 2:18). In that same chapter, in verse 20, we're told that Adam named all the creatures God had made, "but for Adam no suitable helper was found." God had said, "I will make a helper suitable for him" (Gen. 2:18). "So the Lord God caused the man to fall into a deep sleep; and while he was sleeping, he took one of the man's ribs and closed up the place with flesh. Then the Lord God made a woman from the rib he had taken out of the man, and he brought her to the man" (Gen. 2:21-22).

The world has not been the same since! That "helper" has usually been just that. But there are other times when she has been a baffling frustration to the one whom she is supposed to help. Instead of tranquility between husband and wife, there has often been agitation; rather than the home being beautiful, it has often been a battlefield. During an argument with her husband, a wife once said, "Where would you men be if it weren't for us women?" To which the husband replied with apparent irritation, "Probably still in the Garden of Eden!"

I know, I don't know *your* husband—but maybe you don't either! Husbands are strange creatures. When it would be just as easy to hang his coat in the closet, he drapes it across a chair. When there is a hamper provided for the clothes that need to go into the washing machine, he just drops them on the floor and steps over them. After a shower he leaves the wash cloth and towel wadded up in the corner to sour in the heat of the day when you've instructed him time and time again to hang them up to dry. In ten minutes he eats his meals that it took you sixty to prepare and says nothing complimentary at all. Rather he retires to his lounger in front of the TV, picks up the paper, and is all set for the evening while you have to clean it all up. No, I don't know your husband, but they all have some similar characteristics. The questions you're probably asking by now are, "What do I do about it? How do I change him to meet my expectations of what a husband ought to be?"

First, men and women *are* different in many ways, and I hope we'll always keep it that way. God didn't make us alike, but He did make us to be compatible. He did make us equal—but different. Gladys M. Hunt says, "Equality really is not the question. Women are neither inferior to men nor superior to them. We are simply a different creation."[1]

---

[1] Gladys M. Hunt, "Uniquely a Woman," in *The Marriage Affair,* ed. J. Allen Petersen (Wheaton, Ill.: Tyndale House Publishers, 1971), p. 93.

When women expect men to act and react as they do and try to bring their husbands into alignment with their expectations, a collision is usually imminent. In the first place, it's almost an impossible task; and in the second place, it was not intended by our Maker to be that way in the first place. God said, "I will make man a helper" not a competitor, but a complementor. "I will make man one to help make him complete!" In a marriage relationship the husband's nature, personality, and temperament should accentuate those qualities of his wife that are different from his. Likewise, the wife's should supplement those of her husband.

Women are generally more sensitive and more responsive to affectionate consideration than are men. Women usually want to be needed and need to be wanted more deeply than men. Often women, especially those who do not work outside the home, develop a feeling of inadequacy at not being able to be the "perfect wife." Sometimes the result is a slacking off in areas like housekeeping, cooking, laundry, and other duties; probably the very things that should have been given more attention rather than less. I think we need to determine what a "perfect wife" is. Now the ears are perked up! If not, they should be. Well, here it is just the same.

To be perfect in this sense does not necessarily mean to be without fault. Wife, if you try to be faultless in every way, you might as well hang it up! To be perfect in this regard is to fulfill that function for which you were made. Read that last statement again. Think about it! Surely you can do that. God made you for a special reason—to be a "helper" to your husband. A husband cannot be a complete husband unless he has a helper-wife! Our society is so hung up on husbands and wives being independent that we have lost sight of the fact that the Bible clearly outlines that they are to be one—a single unit—not going their own ways, doing their own thing, or doing what they want without regard for the other.

As the wife helps the husband, she should receive her strength and confidence from him and satisfaction from it all. I am not about to say that a wife should not continue to develop her talents and interests or even discover new ones. She should do all that with an eye toward pleasing God, who said to the first wife, "Your desire will be for your husband" (Gen. 3:16). A wife can contend to improve herself without competing with her husband, to contend without being contentious. Contend and contentious sound much alike, but that's where the similarity ends. A husband appreciates a wife's cultivating her innate abilities, for it makes her a better wife; but he does resent her being belligerent about it.

The Bible says, "Wives, submit to your husbands as to the Lord. For the husband is the head of the wife as Christ is the head of the church, his body, of which he is the Savior. Now as the church submits to Christ, so also wives should submit to their husbands in everything" (Eph. 5:22-24). Sometimes wives chafe under the load of this Scripture without cause. When you consider how "Christ is the head of the church," then you understand that the head of the home is to exercise his authority only with love and tenderness—that's how Christ governs the Church.

Possibly some of you think, "My husband will have to change drastically to measure up to this kind of headship!" Well, probably so, most of us do come far short when weighed in the balance of the Bible's guidelines. But have you tried to bring about that change in the right way? Have you always been that same affectionate, delightful, loving girl he married? All too often little petty things have taken their toll on both marriage partners, and without realizing it you have _both_ changed. Once you looked out for the good of the other more than yourself; now you take your mate for granted. He used to hurry around to your side of the car to open the door for you, while you sat, smiling to yourself with pride that he cared that much for your well-being; now that has all ceased. "Well," you say to yourself, "if he is not going to show me the courtesy of opening my car door, I'll stop taking the newspaper to him as he settles into his easy chair! That is one way to get even."

He used to take out the trash every day without fail. Now it's a different story. It began with your having to ask him to do it, then it progressed to your begging him to do it, and now you have to do it yourself if it gets done at all. "Well two can play that game," you decide. "I always work around the plants and flowers around the outside of the house while he mows the grass—now _he_ can just do that himself!" On and on it goes, and where it stops nobody knows. In Solomon's Song of Songs we're told that it's, "the _little_ foxes that ruin the vineyards" (2:15). It always begins with small things, and if they go unchecked, the end result is a complete breakdown of love, respect, and concern and a costly debilitation of the home.

Do you want your husband to be more loving toward you? Have you tried making yourself more lovable? Cecil Osborne says, "If you want to be loved, you must make yourself lovable—not for a day or a week, but on a permanent basis. This may involve a radical change of attitude on your part."[2] Treat him as you want him to treat you; and if it doesn't work the first time, keep at it; and if it still doesn't work, still keep at it; and on and on and on. Nothing constructive is ever accomplished by retaliating in kind when someone does you wrong. "Do to others *as you would have them* do to you" (Lk. 6:31), not as some would put it, "Do unto others *as they do* unto you."

When your husband is more contrary, be more loving. When he is less affectionate toward you, cook his meals a little better. When he acts like he just doesn't care, clean the house a little cleaner. "Do not repay evil for evil. Be careful to do what is right in the eyes of everybody. If it is possible, as far as it depends on you, live at peace with everyone. Do not take revenge, my friends, but leave room for God's wrath, for it is written: 'It is mine to avenge; I will repay,' says the Lord. On the contrary: 'If your enemy is hungry, feed him; if he is thirsty, give him something to drink. In doing this, you will heap burning coals on his head.' Do not be overcome by evil, but overcome evil with good" (Rom. 12:17-21). This Scripture has its place in the marriage. It says to the wife, as well as the husband, "Do all within your power to have a happy home." Concerning the part about heaping burning coals on his head, please be careful not to take it too literally. I knew of a woman who in the heat of an argument took live, hot coals and literally dumped them on her husband's head. I don't think I need to tell you, that's *not* what the Word of God means; nor did it settle the argument.

[2] Cecil Osborne, "When the Honeymoon Is Over," in *The Marriage Affair,* ed. Petersen, p. 97.

You may not always live up to what you know a good wife should be, but keep aiming at it, keep trying. "The Indiana *Bell News* reported that an FBI marksman passed through a small town and saw evidence of amazing shooting accuracy. Painted on trees, walls, fences, and buildings were numerous bull's-eyes with bullet holes in the exact center of each. He searched and found that the marksman was the village idiot. Asked how he could shoot so accurately, he replied, 'I shoot first and draw the circle afterwards.'"[3] Some wives and husbands do the same thing by doing as they please in their home concerning their marriage partner and then trying to find scriptural grounds to support their actions. It is of paramount importance that we *first* go to the Bible and then do as it says. Some of the instructions in the Bible may be "hard to swallow," but if God says it, it is best for all concerned.

"The husband should fulfill his marital duty to his wife, and likewise the wife to her husband. The wife's body does not belong to her alone but also to her husband. In the same way, the husband's body does not belong to him alone but also to his wife" (1 Cor. 7:3-4). The apostle is speaking here about the sexual relationship between husband and wife. Many marital problems either begin or are accelerated by what does or does not go on behind the bedroom door. But the full meaning of the text is not limited to the sexual relationship. It also speaks of a complete commitment between the pair; and that commitment infiltrates every facet of the marriage bond.

Dr. James Hamilton relates the following fable: "A hen

[3] James D. Hamilton, *Directions* (Kansas City, Mo.: Beacon Hill Press, 1976), p. 54.

41

and a hog were traveling together. They passed a church that displayed the sermon subject for the coming Sunday. It read: 'How Can We Help the Poor?' After a moment's reflection the hen ventured, 'I know what we can do! We can give them a ham and egg breakfast.' 'You can say that,' the hog replied 'because for you that's just a contribution, but for me it's total commitment.'"[4]

It is so easy for one partner to say to the other, "It's your fault," or "You're the one who should change." It's much easier than sharing in the commitment of making the marriage work!

Cecil Osborne writes, "It takes a wise and patient wife to make a good husband. They seldom come ready made."[5] The better wife you become, the better husband he'll become. It's amazing how the harder you work at having a better marriage, the more blessing you have in your venture. You might try meeting him at the door with a smile—a smile goes a long way in turning things around—and a warm kiss. It's been a hard day with the kids, the bill collectors, and the flat tire. But please don't hit him with that until *after* he's eaten and begun to calm down from *his* bad day.

"A married woman is concerned," the Word says, ". . . how she can please her husband" (1 Cor. 7:34b). Even if you think you can't please him—give it a try. Too often a wife gets tired of trying and resorts to arguing with him instead. The Bible, however, warns us, "Don't have anything to do with foolish and stupid arguments, because you know they produce quarrels. And the Lord's servant must not quarrel;

[4] Hamilton, *Directions,* p. 55.
[5] Osborne, in *The Marriage Affair,* ed. Petersen, p. 99.

42

instead, he must be kind to everyone, able to teach, not resentful" (2 Tim. 2:23-24). Even though this was written by a veteran preacher to his young protégé, it still applies equally well in the home.

The Bible says, "Wives, submit to your husbands, as is fitting in the Lord" (Col. 3:18). This comes under the heading of "Rules for Christian Households" and says that submission is a necessary part of those households. Note that verse 25 of the same chapter says that with God "there is no favoritism." What God expects from the wife toward her husband, He expects from the husband toward Him. But, what if the husband is not constant to keep his part of the bargain with the Lord? The wife is still held responsible for her actions and reactions toward her husband; he'll have to answer to God for his disobedience. "So then, each of us will give an account of himself to God" (Rom. 14:12). This should quiet the statement, "But my husband doesn't do what he is supposed to do; he doesn't keep his part of the agreement!" Wife, *you* are accountable for *your* part of the marriage responsibilities according to the Word of God; he will have to answer for his doings.

I once saw a sign in an office that read, "Eat a live frog the first thing every morning and that's the worst thing you'll have to face all day." I really don't think that's the solution for having to put up with a husband who is considerably less than delightful. If you want your relationship with your husband to improve, remember some of the things you did to get him in the first place.

Were you always careful to look your best when he was with you? Did you take care to keep your weight down to attractive proportions? Did you let him see you running around with you in curlers and in a shabby housecoat? Did you always complain to him about his annoying idiosyncrasies? Did you ever show extra kindness when he was curt with you? He was your sweetheart then, is he now? Is he still your lover or just your "old man"?

As you pack for your husband to go on a business trip, do you ever put little love notes in various places where he's sure to find them? Put one in a sock, in an undershirt, or maybe in his coat pocket. If you want to, you can be very imaginative as to where they go. I know from personal experience that those strategically placed "love notes" will make his heart beat a little faster when he opens that suitcase in an empty motel room and realizes it was packed with love. To tell the truth of the matter, he'll wish you were there. Oh yes, you might expect him to call you shortly after he checks in.

I heard of a wife who packed love notes in her husband's lunch. What about a love letter for lunch? It makes great dessert! If things haven't gone too well at home for the last couple of days, it is a good way to say "I'm sorry."

When you were first married, did you take special care to fold his freshly washed clothes and then neatly place them in his drawer, with everything in just the right place? Do you still take that same care, or do you throw them in just any way or even leave them in a basket for him to hunt and sort out every morning before work? That kind of an arrangement is not very conducive to creating in him a keen desire to hurry home as soon as the whistle blows. Wouldn't it be great, wives, to have your husband leave for work impatient to get back home to his bride! Although Revelation 2:4—"You have forsaken your first love"—was written to a church about her love toward Christ, this message is often applied to the human union of matrimony, considering that the husband-wife relationship is like that between Christ and his bride, the church.

Is your love toward your husband as alive today as when you took the vows at the altar? If it isn't, you need to do everything within your power to revive it! "Be kind and compassionate to one another, forgiving each other, *just as in Christ God forgave you*" (Eph. 4:32). That's a big order—but you can fill it! How about beginning by saying something like, "Honey, I'm sorry, I've acted selfishly, please forgive me." As you ask your mate to forgive you, you must at the same time forgive him; and to forgive him means to begin to treat him with more tender kindness and more warmhearted compassion.

Together you must ask God for His help and guidance in the matter of homemaking and then work His plan in the Bible into the marriage.

A man's house is his fortress in a warring world,
where a woman's hand buckles on his armor in the
morning and soothes his fatigue and wounds at night.[6]

Frank Crane

[6] *The Marriage Affair,* ed. Petersen, p. 92.

chapter five

But you don't Know my wife!

"Husbands, love your wives, just as Christ loved the church and gave himself up for her to make her holy, cleansing her by the washing with water through the word, and to present her to himself as a radiant church, without stain or wrinkle or any other blemish, but holy and blameless. In this same way, husbands ought to love their wives as their own bodies. He who loves his wife loves himself" (Eph. 5:25-28). ". . . each one of you also must love his wife as he loves himself, and the wife must respect her husband" (Eph. 5:33).

What a profound statement! Husbands, take note—God is talking to you through this, His Word—the Holy Bible. "But you don't know my wife!" you might contend. But God didn't say, "love your wife if she's perfect," but rather, "love your wives, just as Christ loved the church."

You might ask, "What is the perfect wife?" I suppose there are as many different answers to the question as there are men asking the question. Each of us has his own idea of what a wife should be or should not be. Thus, I won't even try to outline the qualities of the "perfect" wife, since I'm not sure what they would be. Nonetheless, I want us to consider our wives in the light of the Word of God and what He says our actions and reactions should be to come into harmony with Him *and* with our spouses. Since God is the author of the marriage and the home, by following His outline there should be harmony in the home.

One fellow said he knew his wife was an angel since she was always up in the air, harping about not having an earthly thing to wear. This was his way of saying his "angel" was hard to please.

So what if your wife leaves her hosiery dripping wet in the bathroom, does not have your dinner ready when you arrive at the front door tired and hungry, and occasionally forgets to have a clean, freshly pressed shirt for you to wear to church on Sunday. What are you to do about it? You *are* the head of the house, you know! The answer—love her.

The apostle Peter said, "Above all, love each other deeply, because love covers over a multitude of sins" (1 Pet. 4:8). If the husband loves his wife as Christ loves the church, she may not be perfect but his love will overlook the imperfections. Let him that is without imperfections cast the first stone.

In some homes the husband and wife fight only once a day but it begins the first thing in the morning and ends the last thing at night—without meal breaks. God's plan for the husband-wife relationship is not a survival of the fittest nor is it an endurance test. God's design for marriage partners is:

50

". . . at the beginning the Creator 'made them male and female,' and said, 'For this reason a man will leave his father and mother and be united to his wife, and the two will become one flesh.' So they are no longer two, but one" (Mt. 19:5-6).

God's calculations are different from human ones; who ever heard of one plus one adding up to one? In the beginning of creation God took one, Adam, and from him made two, Adam and Eve, and in marriage He reunites the two into one. The Word of God indicates that when a man mistreats his wife, he is harming himself. When he fights with his wife, he is fighting himself. When he doesn't love his wife, the source of the problem goes deeper than disdain for his wife; it has its root in his contempt for something he sees in himself. The Scripture that says, "He who loves his wife loves himself" (Eph. 5:28b) is also saying, "He who hates his wife hates himself."

The husband might say, "But she's so different from me!" In reality those differences probably brought you together. If both halves of the marriage unit were the same it would be impossible to mesh the halves into one whole, harmonious union. The differences in likes and dislikes should complement those of the mate. It should not be a matter of saying, "Our marriage was made in heaven," when in reality it is being destroyed on earth. I'm not sure about marriages being made in heaven; I believe they were ordained by God, but they must be "made" to work right here in the nitty-gritty of everyday life.

Peter was talking to the wives about some of their responsibilities in the marriage union when he says, "Husbands, in the same way be considerate as you live with your wives, and treat them with respect as the weaker partner and as heirs with you of the gracious gift of life, so that nothing will hinder your prayers" (1 Pet. 3:7). The New American Standard version puts it this way, ". . . live with your wives in an understanding way." Most of the time men have difficulty understanding their wives. They are often so different in almost every way. Sometimes when the husband thinks he has her figured out, she changes—her mood has changed or she's changed her mind.

Take, for instance, some wives' shopping habits. Usually when a man goes to buy a suit or a pair of pants, he knows about what he wants and where to buy it—it's a simple matter to him—no big deal. But when a woman sets out to find a dress or pair of shoes, it's often quite another matter. Complications usually set in since she can't find a dress just the right shade of gray to go with the gray purse and shoes she already has. As you tag along from one store to another, your patience is stretched almost to the breaking point. Finally, after the day is exhausted and you are too, this test of endurance comes to an end with your wife going back to the very first store and buying the first dress she looked at, or perhaps she decides to buy a different color dress, which necessitates a new purse and shoes to match, or perhaps you go home exhausted from the marathon and your wife bought neither dress nor purse nor shoes. Then to cap it all off, she says something like, "I really wish I had bought that second dress I tried on—maybe I'll go back tomorrow and get it if it's still there." You can't even remember what the second dress looked like!

I realize the scenario above is somewhat exaggerated and the characters somewhat stereotyped, but I believe it serves to clarify the point at hand: "Husbands, live with your wives in an understanding way," no matter how much your patience is tried!

How, then, do husbands live with their wives in an understanding way? He can try to realize that the things that are most important to his wife are often not all that important to him. However, he should treat her with respect, respecting her judgments, tastes, and priorities. When the Word of God says that she is the weaker partner, it does not in any way intimate that she is weaker in mind and understanding. It is talking about the physical. Thus husbands shouldn't treat their wives as though they were weak-minded, but respect them and even try more to understand those things about their wives they don't understand.

Your wife is an heir "with you of the gracious gift of life." You should be in the Christian walk *together*. Union with the Lord is more than mere emotional ups and downs; so our union with our mate does not depend on emotions alone. Real, God-oriented love must be deeper than our passing feelings. If your life in Christ is based only on how you feel at the moment, you're in trouble. There are some days when we just don't have the feelings that we have when everything is going well. It's at those times in our lives that we must say within ourselves, "Praise the Lord, anyhow." Sometimes the "feeling" is absent for days and even weeks. The secret is to not give up. The same applies in our marraige relationship; there are times when our feelings are not as pronounced for our mate as at other times. Pressures of life, the job, the bills, sickness, and many other things can cause our sensibilities toward our mates to be dulled. This in no way indicates that we no longer love our spouse or even cease to care for her and her emotional and physical well-being. It *does* mean that there is a potential problem lurking in the background, ready to invade the sanctity of the marriage bond, and that immediate attention must be given to solving the problems.

Howard G. Hendricks cites Dr. James A. Peterson, professor of sociology at the University of Southern California and a foremost authority on marriage and family life, as having "completed an extensive study of couples who had been married between 20 and 35 years. His conclusion was that only six couples out of every hundred were satisfied and fulfilled by their marriage relationship."[1] Hendricks goes on to say, "The greatest reason for failure is unrealistic expectations."[2]

In the beginning when God created the human race, He said, "It is not good for the man to be alone" (Gen. 2:18). The Lord formed woman to be a "helper suitable for man." Do you suppose men expect their wives to be more than helpers? Maybe they tend to lay the blame on them when things go wrong. It seems that Adam began this tactic when he said to God, "The woman you put here with me—*she* gave me some fruit from the tree, and I ate it" (Gen. 3:12). This was the same Adam who had just said, upon seeing Eve for the first time, "Wow! She's just what I've been looking for!"

[1] Howard G. Hendricks, *Say It with Love* (Wheaton, Ill.: Victor Books, 1972), p. 80. Used by permission of the publisher, a division of SP Publications, Inc.

[2] Ibid.

Many a man has had the same experience in his own "paradise" when he meets the woman who becomes his wife and he says, "You were meant for me!" "You're just what I need!" and on and on the platitudes go. When problems come and the honeymoon is over, he sings a new song: "If *you* would just change, things would be better." We always like to blame someone else for our misfortunes and mistakes. Years ago whenever we would travel, our daughters would take coloring books and crayons along in the car to keep themselves busy. Many times when I would go around a corner or hit a bump in the road, one of them would say from the back seat, "Daddy, look what you made me do!" They had colored out of the lines, and it was daddy's fault. Is it possible that in our marriages blame is too often *given* rather than *taken*?

Woman was taken from the rib of man; not from his head to lord it over him, nor from his feet to be trampled on by him, but from his side to be equal with him, from under his arm to be protected by him, and from close to his heart to be loved by him.

Our marriage partner must be courted. *To court* is an old-fashioned term meaning "to woo" and "to pursue a lover." Postmarriage courtship is as important as premarriage courtship, if not more so. Too often a man will say, "I have her now, what's the need to continue pursuing?" When this happens, the last-of-the-big-spenders boyfriend becomes the skinflint husband. The same man who thought nothing of spending a good portion of his week's paycheck on the apple of his eye now thinks in a different way. He forgets that the very things that caused the sparkle in dating need to be continued in marriage. After all, it's the same woman, and he should have the same goal—to win her affections.

Those dinners by candlelight in a romantic atmosphere are as important to her now as they were then, even if she is the Mrs. Some budgets don't allow for much of this, but "where there is a will there is a way." Maybe you can meet for lunch in a nice restaurant or maybe even have breakfast together away from home where the two of you can talk and be alone together. There is nothing quite like husband and wife leaving the children and the cares of home for a change of scenery. A couple of days and nights in a motel, just the two of you, can do wonders for a marriage. It helps to keep the sparkle in the marriage. The sparkle always goes out before the marriage dies.

I suppose husbands are the world's best forgetters. They forget to bring home that loaf of bread that their wives called the office about. They forget to pick up the children from school when it's raining; most of all, they so easily forget birthdays, anniversaries, and other important times and events that are extremely important to their wives.

When we got married, my bride chose yellow roses for the wedding. For several years after that I brought her yellow roses on our anniversary. That was several years ago. I haven't brought her a yellow rose in I don't know when. Maybe it's because they got so expensive I thought we couldn't afford them. I hope it's not because I no longer care; I do bring her something to show her I still remember.

A friend of mine lived in another country where roses were very inexpensive, and on their anniversary he always sent his wife a red rose for each year of their marriage. On their thirty-seventh anniversary she was in the United States while he was detained on foreign soil, but he still remembered their anniversary. He got word to a friend to have the thirty-seven roses delivered to her, not knowing the high price of roses in the United States. When he got the bill for nearly $100, he realized that love is not cheap! What an impression it made on his wife to know that he missed her as much as she missed him! It doesn't have to be $100 worth of roses, but I think most of us can do better if we really care and try.

Remember this, if the marriage relationship is not courted after the wedding and while the children are growing up, there will be little if anything left when the last child leaves the nest. Husband, if you plan to have a happy home when it's just you and your "bride," after the little ones are no longer under foot, you had better build a lasting relationship with your wife now. Too many wait until it is too late. Nor can your entire marriage be built on the children, for the time will come when they will begin their own home, and what will you have left?

There must be truth and openness in a lasting marriage. Marriage is a partnership, and if one partner does his or her own thing without at least consulting the other—there is danger ahead! He wants a new car, and she says, "We don't need one, we can't afford it." What do you do? You both think you are right, and you both think the other really doesn't understand the situation. I can't give you a pat answer here, but I do know that if the husband comes in with a new car and new payments all on his own, he has not treated his wife with consideration.

Remember 1 Peter 3:7, the husband is to respect his

wife, so that nothing will hinder his prayers. An unfavorable relationship at home *will* hinder prayer!

Paul, speaking to the Corinthian church concerning worship in the church was referring to their law and custom about wives remaining silent in church, but he went on to say, "If they want to inquire about something, they should ask their own husbands at home" (1 Cor. 14:35). The emphasis here should not be on the custom of the time of wives keeping silent in public, but rather on the fact that since God has prescribed that the husband should be the head of the wife, the husband has the awesome responsibility to be the spiritual leader as well.

Again and again we see the responsibility for the spiritual welfare of the home shifted to the wife. In the Church there are far more women actively engaged in the work of the Lord than there are men. Often it's the wife and children who go to Sunday school; the husband sleeps in and then rounds out the day reading the hefty Sunday paper, absorbing a massive dose of football, and finally, being completely worn out, gropes his way back to bed to get rested up for another week at hard labor. The husband has delegated his responsibility concerning spiritual leadership to his wife, who usually gets the blame if the children don't turn out right.

The Bible says that the husband is to give the religious instruction in his home, and he must not relinquish this privilege to anyone, not even his wife. Sometimes husbands have the idea that it's not manly or masculine to get involved with "religion." For the record, let me remind you that it takes a *real* man to be the head of the home as God intends! This includes the spiritual head as well.

There was never a more masculine man than Jesus Christ, who took unmerited scorn, beatings, humiliation, and finally death with criminals without retaliation. It was a real man who said to the Father from the cross, "Forgive them, for they do not know what they are doing" (Lk. 23:34). It was a real man who was struck without striking back. It was a real man who was spit upon without a word in return. This same Jesus felt the sting of agony in sorrow when, at His friend's death, He wept. These things did not diminish His masculinity, but augmented it.

You don't have to be a sissy to show love and concern. I believe a man ought to be a man in every regard and this includes a man's emotions. Yes, men have emotions too. Paul reminds us that, "We have this treasure in jars of clay to show that this all-surpassing power is from God and not from us" (2 Cor. 4:7). The "jar of clay" is the human frame—being human—humanness. God knows husbands are human. Notice Paul said, "jars of clay," not cracked pots; there *is* a difference! Husbands, assume the role of the man of the house in spiritual matters!

The question is often asked, "Do you think prayer will solve all the problems of the marriage?" Remember what the apostle James had to say about the matter of "faith and works." He said, "Faith without deeds is useless" (Jas. 2:20b). Husbands and wives should pray together, but there must also be some action on the part of both to see God's plan work. In Bob Mumford's little book, *Living Happily Ever After,* he relates a problem that arose between himself and his wife, and they decided to pray about it. He says, "'O God, change that woman,' went up my impassioned plea." "From

59

the next room came an equally sincere petition, 'O God, change that man You gave me.'"[3]

What's God to do? God hears those fervent cries and will give the answer when husband, as well as wife, is willing to obey Him even if it means some changing in their own attitudes and actions. It is easy to say, "Lord, change her" or "Lord, change him," but much more difficult to pray with a sincere heart, "Lord, change me."

Marriage is give and take but it can't always be the same one giving and the same one taking. A husband can never be oversensitive to the needs and hurts of his wife. Wives are usually more sensitive and more easily hurt than their counterparts, and husbands should do all within their power to try to better understand that fact. The Bible says, "If it is possible, as far as it depends on you, live at peace with everyone" (Rom. 12:8). We have not done our part, husbands, to have a tranquil home until we have made every concession, extended every overture of love, and made every attempt at reconciliation as far as it depends on us. God help us to do a better job of it!

Love must be acted out in the marriage relationship, but it must be verbalized too, more often than it is in most cases. It is hard for many men, me included, to say, "I love you." But wives love to hear it. Most women thrive on love, not just in practice but in being told on a regular basis. Husbands are often too much like the man who, when asked how often he told his wife he loved her, replied, "I told her twenty years ago, and when that changes she'll be the first to know." I

---

[3] Bob Mumford, *Living Happily Ever After* (Old Tappan, N.J.: Fleming H. Revell Company, 1973), p. 21.

realize that I fall far short in this category, but I guess an honest confession is good for the soul. I have resolved with God's help to do better. How about you? Don't you think your wife would like to hear those three little words more often?

Love must be unconditional. The Bible says we are to love our wives just like Christ loved the Church—that's unconditional love. He gave His life for the Church—that's giving *everything*. His mandate to the husband is not to love his wife as long as she pleases you or as long as she keeps the house clean, cooks your meals, washes your clothes, and cares for your children. It is to love her unconditionally. It may result in helping with the dishes or vacuuming when you don't really feel like it because she has had a rough day. When a wife works outside the home, the chores of the house should be divided so that the husband does his share.

Unconditional love doesn't cover up a deep hurt that can fester into a real sore spot in the union. Husbands sometimes hurt their wives, often without even knowing it at the time. Men are often crude when they should be gentle. When the hurt is realized, *that* is the time to take necessary steps to heal the hurt. Most wife abuse is not physical but emotional. Unless forgiveness is asked and proper actions are taken to promote healing, emotional hurts may take longer to heal than physical ones.

Referring again to the Bible, we find the admonitions: "Love the Lord your God with all your heart and with all your soul and with all your mind" (Mt. 22:37) and "Love your neighbor as yourself" (v. 39). I once heard someone say, "How are you supposed to love someone you don't even like?" That's a good question! Husband, your wife should be someone you "like." She should be your best friend. You should adapt to her likes and dislikes as much as possible. Maybe you like to fish and she doesn't—she would rather go on a picnic. What do you do? How about a fishing-picnic? My wife doesn't care at all about fishing; she won't even eat fish. But we have often gone on fishing-picnics, where the girls and I would fish, usually without much success, and we would all fry and eat the catch-of-the-day, except Mom, who would fix a hamburger. At least the whole family was together enjoying each other.

When Matthew says, "a man will leave his father and mother and be united to his wife" (19:5), that is just what God meant. To leave father and mother does not mean to forsake them but it does mean that a man accepts his wife's burned toast, unseasoned vegetables, and pork chops that are not quite done, without telling her how good a cook his mom is. One husband said, "I know I'm my wife's idol—every meal she presents me with a burnt offering!" Maybe your wife is not the best cook or the most immaculate housekeeper, but give her time—she'll learn. I can hear it now, "We've been married twenty years and she hasn't learned yet!" Well, friend, you should have adjusted to it by now; and a continual "harping" on it won't change the matter at this point. Can you imagine the impact on her self-esteem when, after a meal that was less than satisfying, you reflect back on the good meals you had at home. It certainly is not encouragement. Surely there was something about the meal that merited a compliment: "Honey, you sure can make good coffee."

People need to hear a sincere expression of praise from time to time. If your wife looks especially pretty, tell her so. If the house has the look and smell of a full day of hard work in cleaning—the windows look clearer than you've noticed before, the kitchen is spotless, and everything seems to be in its place—compliment her. Too often we are quick to complain and slow to compliment. There was a song years ago that said, "Accentuate the positive, eliminate the negative." That's pretty good advice for all to accept. If you try it and your wife faints, be patient, she'll revive.

The Bible says that by loving our wives as Christ loved the Church and as we love ourselves, we'll be better husbands, and our spouses will be better wives. Try it!

chapter six

Help!
I'm a parent

Parents spend their children's childhood years wondering how their children will turn out and their adolescent years wondering when they will turn in. Listen to these comments made by parents: "I give my kids everything they want and *this* is the thanks I get!" "When I was young I couldn't act like that and get by with it!" "It seems to me the younger generation is going completely to pot!" "If that was my kid, I'd wear him out!"

Did you ever hear any of these statements or variations that convey the same message? They all point out that there are times in the lives of children when they need correction and that much of the time parents just don't know what to do about it. God's Word to us says, "The rod of correction imparts wisdom, but a child left to itself disgraces his mother" (Prov. 29:15). And it also says, "Discipline your son, and he will give you peace; he will bring delight to your soul" (Prov.

29:17). Also, "Discipline your son, for in that there is hope" (Prov. 19:18). Although these Scriptures speak of sons, they mean daughters as well.

The Bible clearly lets us know that our responsibility as parents includes correction. Some children need more of the "rod" than others, but there are few children who do not need any correction at all along this pathway we call growing up. Many are the instructions in the Word that have to do with parental discipline, but not one of them indicates that correction should be administered without the good of the child at heart or merely for the satisfaction of the parent. I've seen parents harshly discipline their offspring with an attitude of having the last say or of getting even. When the child is corrected in a manner other than that outlined in God's Word, the end result is unsatisfactory or even disastrous.

We had just begun our family and had moved into a new home in a nice, respectable neighborhood where the young families all seemed to have at least one child. All of the boys and girls were very well behaved, played well together, and seemed to enjoy one another's company, *except Charlie*. Charlie was a hyperactive little guy about five years old. He lived across the street from us and sometimes played with our then three-year-old daughter, Star. We soon learned that Mother had to keep an eye on Charlie to see what he was up to at all times. I guess the first experience with Charlie was when he and our little girl were looking at a small bush by the side of our house. The bush had brightly colored "fruit," or so it seemed, all over it. Some were red, some were green, some were purple, some yellow and blue—it was a very attractive and intriguing little bush. On that eventful day, my wife heard Star crying and even screaming at the top of her voice. When she got there, she saw that she had something in her mouth that she was trying to get out. You see, the "fruit" of that little bush turned out to be the hottest peppers I'd ever tasted. Charlie had told Star that the little pretty things were good to eat, so she tried one. One was all it took. She began to cry and rub her eyes and the pepper got in her eyes and on her face and everywhere it touched it hurt. Charlie began to quicken his pace toward home when he saw my wife coming. He knew what the bright little peppers really were, and he had wanted to pull a fast one on the little three-year-old.

Charlie began to take things that did not belong to him; he even went to the convenience store down the block, "robbed" toys, and ran home with the clerk chasing him.

One day our neighbors came home from work and found their house flooded with about three inches of water. You guessed it, Charlie had turned their water hose on and stood at their back door and watered the inside of the house with three inches of water. On and on it went with "Charlie the menace," as he became known in the neighborhood.

The most Charlie's mother ever did in her feeble attempt at correction was just to yell, "Charlie, I don't know what to do with you!" As far as I could see, she never did anything with him. I often wondered what ever happened to Charlie. I'm afraid that if he didn't get some better correction somewhere along the way, he's in a peck of trouble today.

I realize that some children are more active and harder to correct than others but at least Charlie's parents could have tried. Just to yell at "that kid" is not godly correction. There is a time to apply the "board of education," and the Lord has provided a portion of the anatomy for that purpose. I've heard parents that often threaten punishment without ever delivering it. The youngsters soon know whether or not they will keep their promise.

I grew up in Indiana where some fine peaches grow. If you know anything about peach trees, you know that they have exceedingly keen little branches that, when cut from the tree, make a very lively switch. We had one of those lovely peach trees behind our house. I really forget whether or not it ever had peaches on it, but I vividly remember it as a "switch factory." On occasion, actually many occasions, Mother would take a quick trip to the "factory" and, stepping lively as she held the base of the branch in her left hand, would strip the leaves off with her right hand and head back for the house where my brother and I (one or both) waited for "judgment."

My parents didn't believe in spanking trousers, so down the trousers would come, and where the pants had been there disciplinary action would take place. When the trousers were pulled up and the switch put away, the memory lingered on and on. But I can honestly say that I never knew my parents to administer punitive action except from a heart of love and concern.

Since I have become a parent, I know what is meant by the expression, almost worn out now, "This hurts me more than it hurts you." When love is the motive for correction and the parent knows it is for the good of the child, it is still like correcting part of himself or herself. As a tree must be straightened at times to grow straight and tall, so must children have their course realigned whenever they tend to get off track.

Children must always know what they're being corrected for; they must understand the parents' values that make that correction necessary. The parent must be consistent too. The youngster sees and understands more about your motives and love, or lack of love, than you can realize. You can correct them without losing their respect. It is of utmost importance that your children's respect is won and maintained in early years to be preserved in later years.

Dr. James Dobson, assistant professor of pediatrics at the University of Southern California School of Medicine, says in his book, *Dare to Discipline,* "If you want your child to accept your values when he reaches his teen years, then you must be worthy of his respect during his younger days. When a child can successfully defy his parents during his first fifteen years, laughing in their faces and stubbornly flouting their authority, he develops a natural contempt for them." ". . . Later he is likely to demonstrate his disrespect in a more open manner."[1]

The writer of the Proverbs said, while talking about a good wife and mother, "Her children arise and call her blessed" (31:28). What an epilogue to a parent's life—that the children would rise up and call her blessed! Moms and Dads, do everything you can to bring this about!

[1] James Dobson, *Dare to Discipline* (Wheaton, Ill.: Tyndale House Publishers, 1970), p. 26.

*They do not love
who do not show their love.*[2]

Shakespeare

Sometimes it is not correction that the younger one needs; it might be good Christian advice. Questions that may seem elementary to you may be of great importance to the young inquirer. Treat them as such. A child or teenager knows when you are just giving an answer to get rid of him or her or when you are just making light of the situation. If your children get the right kind of response from you, the parent, they are more likely to come to you with the real "heavy" issues of life. Nothing is quite as rewarding as having your son or daughter come to you, even when they are grown, for advice and understanding. It can only happen if you build that trust and respect while they're young. You may not always have the right answers, but you can always try your best. If neither you nor they know the answer, maybe, just maybe you can work it out together. Parent, take time for your son or your daughter! You'll be glad you did.

A young father and mother were standing in front of me in a cafeteria line recently. They had a young son (about ten months old), and the father was putting him in a rolling high chair while his four-year-old daughter was getting somewhat in his way. He finally asked her to move, and with a sad look she said to her mother, "I was only trying to walk with Daddy." That brought to mind the many times when I was

[2] Quoted in *The Marriage Affair,* ed. J. Allen Petersen (Wheaton, Ill.: Tyndale House Publishers, 1971), p. 210.

busy with something and my daughters would come to me without saying a word and sometimes get in my way. When I'd ask them what they wanted, they'd just say, "Nothing, I just want to be with you, Daddy." I guess that's about the best feeling a father can have. Mothers and fathers, create an atmosphere around your young ones that will make them "just want to be with Daddy and Mommy."

I believe in all our dealings with our children we must do at least three things: be kind, be firm, and be fair. I know that many children are growing up with just one parent, but when there are two parents, they *must* always agree concerning dealings with the children. *Never* argue in front of them about their correction or advice. Those things should be settled behind closed doors.

In the Bible we read, "Fathers, do not embitter your children, or they will become discouraged" (Col. 3:21). For *embitter* the KJV says *provoke,* and the NASV reads *exasperate.* Whichever word you want to use, the meaning is to do what you do with a heart of love. I almost cringe when I hear a parent say, "I don't care what you want, you'll do as I say and like it!" Too often the parent has not given a satisfactory reason for doing as he or she says. The child needs to know *why* it is in his or her best interest to do as the parent says. An answer such as, "just because" is not good enough if you want your child to respect your judgment now and later on in life.

As parents, we often fail to answer questions that are rudimental to us, but whose answers have not yet been learned by our children. For instance, when Mom and Dad go to church, they should expect the whole family to go unless they are sick or otherwise legitimately unable to go. But to say to the child who does not want to go that you go and ask no questions about it is usually not enough. There are some children who will go without ever asking, "Do I have to go today?" But others who ask that question need a valid answer to the question. *You* know that the writer of Hebrews said, "Let us not give up meeting together, as some are in the habit of doing" (10:25), but do your children know what it says in the Bible about going to church?

You know that there are some things that are harmful to the body and soul of any person and that God's Word says, "Keep yourself pure" (1 Tim. 5:22b), but do your children know that? Do they realize that "the wages of sin is death" (Rom. 6:23) and that "The sins of some men are obvious, reaching the place of judgment ahead of them; the sins of others trail behind them" (1 Tim. 5:24).

Too often we may fail to realize that the Bible truths we learned long ago and have heard so often are new to our children. Parents have been young but the children in our care have not been older. Many of the lessons we have learned from the Bible and the experiences of life should be taught to our children.

It's better for them to be taught gently by parents who love them than to have to learn the answers to life's questions from the sometimes harshness of experience. Whether the answers come directly from the Bible or come from years of living and common sense, it is our God-given duty to train and teach our own.

Those whom God has put in our care and keeping will get shortchanged if we fail to impress these truths indelibly on their hearts and minds! As a parent we can throw up our hands and complain, "I am to the end of myself; I don't know what to do with that kid!" or we can turn to the Bible and follow its admonition: "Do not exasperate your children; instead, bring them up in the training and instruction of the Lord" (Eph. 6:4). When you don't know where to turn, turn to the Bible! "Trust in the Lord with all your heart and lean not on your own understanding" (Prov. 3:5).

Some parents take the coward's way out by saying in word and deed, "I'll wait until they're old enough to decide for themselves about God, the church, and other religious matters." I've always thought it strange that those who say that don't say it when it comes to the matter of going to school, brushing their teeth, mowing the lawn, or taking a bath. Remember, "A child left to itself disgraces his mother" (Prov. 29:15).

> *There are two freedoms:*
> *the false where one is free to do what he likes,*
> *and the true where he is free to do what he ought.*[3]
>
> Charles Kingsley

"Pray continually" (1 Thess. 5:17). What good advice for parents! When should you begin to pray for your children? As soon as you become a parent! When should you stop pray-

---

[3] Quoted in *The Marriage Affair*, ed. Petersen, p. 229.

ing for your children? They never outgrow the need for their parents' prayers! I heard an old man praying in church the other day. He said, "O Lord, you know we have a boy out west somewhere; please seek him out and speak to his heart, he needs You!" That impassioned cry from the heart of a father for a son who was probably sixty years old or more, but who was still "his boy," did not go unheard by his heavenly Father. He had prayed that prayer many times before, but he would not give up now. He still loved and cared! The Word says, "Train a child in the way he should go, and when he is old he will not turn from it" (Prov. 22:6). This does not mean that children will never go against godly teaching or that they will never go their own way instead of God's way. But it does mean that if we train them right when they are young, we have every right to expect God to continue to draw on that early training to once again get to their hearts.

I was called upon recently to conduct the funeral of a godly minister who had preached for more than fifty years and had, with his good wife, reared three daughters. Just before the funeral I was looking through his old Bible to see his "tracks", that is, where he had been in the Word and his notations of answered prayers throughout his many years. In the back of that old Book there was a note to "the one who preaches my funeral."

With keen interest I read what was obviously written for me although it was pasted in the back of that Bible many years before I met this man of God. It read something like this: "At my funeral please tell my daughters that there has not been a day that has passed that their mother and I have not prayed for them. We have always loved them and even after they established their own homes we continued to pray that God would guide them in every area of their lives. Please tell them that Mom and I plan to meet them 'just inside the Eastern Gate!'" What better legacy could a parent leave children!

Children need to have good memories of their home and their parents. The only way for them to have good memories is to establish a good home and good relationships while they are young. You don't have to have everything to give your family good memories. I was born during the Depression. My Dad made about a dollar and a half a day. (I don't think things got any better financially after I arrived, either.) In those days, we didn't have a lot of "things," but we still had each other. I still have so many good memories of our home and family life together.

I remember hearing a teenage boy in a Sunday school class, when asked what he thought a certain lesson was about, say, "It means that some people are *more unfortunate than we are.*" This boy was from a broken home where there was not much love or anything else except quarreling. He felt deprived of many of the things that most teenagers just accept as normal benefits of life and the home. His statement reflected his apparent unhappiness; he said, "more un-fortunate," when most other boys would have said, "less fortunate."

It's a healthy situation for young people to have jobs to do around home. They shouldn't expect to be paid for every little thing they do either. There are certain chores that everyone in the home must assume. When our daughters were growing up there was usually a list on the refrigerator door that outlined the duties of each for the week. Of course, the youngest was not expected to do as much as the older ones. When they had a part-time job outside the home, they were not expected to take on the same chores they would have had if there were no outside jobs. Mom tried her best to be as fair and equitable as possible with all four of them, although at times they didn't realize it.

When children learn responsibility at home they are more apt to face up to the reality of responsibility in the work-a-day world. We do our children an injustice when we shield them from any responsibility in the home. I've seen parents abuse this, but I believe that a child's training is not complete without some teaching on being responsible in their world. "If a man is lazy, the rafters sag; if his hands are idle, the house leaks" (Eccles. 10:18). If they don't learn to be industrious at home, where will they learn it?

The Bible says concerning those who are mentally and physically able to work, "If a man will not work, he shall not eat" (2 Thess. 3:10).

There once was a man who used to go around the country speaking to vast audiences on the subject, "Ten Rules for Rearing Children" before he had any children of his own. A few months after his first child was born, he changed his subject title to "Ten Suggestions for Rearing Children." A couple of years later another child came into his home and again his topic title changed; this time it was "Ten Hints on Rearing

Children." Finally twins arrived in his home, and the man cancelled all his speaking engagements. I don't have all the answers and neither do you; nor does anyone else. But the Word of God says "If any of you lacks wisdom, he should ask God, who gives generously to all without finding fault, and it will be given to him" (Jas. 1:5). That's exactly what every parent should do when he or she is hit with the realization, "I'm a parent! Help!"

chapter seven

My parents just don't understand me

By the time we get our parents, they're so old it's almost impossible to change them! That's the attitude, if not the words, of many a young person concerning the child-parent relationship. So what's new? I suppose it has always been that way to some degree.

Genesis relates that Eve "gave birth to Cain. . . . Later she gave birth to his brother Abel" (4:1-2). These two sons received the same instruction concerning what God expected of them in the way of sacrifices. Verses 6 and 7 of the same chapter indicate that they both knew what the Lord required of them; but one rebelled. He rebelled against God, but he also rebelled against his parents' teaching and against his own brother. I guess this was the first breakdown in communication between child and parents. We have nothing recorded that says that they had a fight or even argued over the thing, but all indications point to the fact that this rebellion did not begin over night but was some time in the making.

There was jealousy between brothers that ended in the death of Abel but that probably began at the breakfast table. Reading between the lines, I can almost hear Cain say, "But I can't see why God won't accept my sacrifice the same as Abel's since it was from the work of my hands the same as his was. The only difference is that his was flesh and mine was fruit!"

Dad said, "Now son just think back about the instructions your mother and I have given you direct from God Himself; it must be a blood sacrifice. God doesn't love you any less than He loves your brother, but He does expect you to follow His directives to the letter." "But it's not fair," came the reply, "you and mother are just taking up for Abel because you love him more than you love me." Eve finally gets to speak, "Son, we love you both the same; we just want you to follow God's will for your life."

So, Cain decided that the way to settle this family dispute was to do away with what he thought to be the source of the problem—his brother. Verse 8 tells us that he did just that.

The above may sound somewhat "earthy," but I think people haven't changed all that much. These kinds of things happen today; usually they don't have the same result, but the problem of communication is still there. It was there when my father was a boy; it was there when I was a boy; and it is there with my offspring.

Adam and Eve were talking to their sons from first-hand experience with God since they had both walked and talked with Him. Parents since then have not had the same privilege of getting their orders from above in exactly the same manner, but God still gives instructions concerning His will for families to parents who are willing to listen. And young people still reject or at least ignore it at times.

I am not about to say that parents "know-it-all," but the Bible gives us, parent and sibling alike, divine information on how to live together in harmony.

The fifth commandment gives us the first suggestion concerning God's feeling on the matter: "Honor your father and your mother" (Exod. 20:12). This is backed up in the New Testament by the words, "which is the first commandment with a promise." And the promise? "That it may go well with you and that you may enjoy long life on the earth" (Eph. 6:2-3).

"Children, obey your parents in the Lord, for this is right" (Eph. 6:1). The term used here for *obey* is different from that used when wives are told to obey, or submit to, their husbands. It comes from a word that carries with it the meaning "to hear," which gives us the idea that God is speaking about "listening" or "giving attention to" our parents. This says that children have the moral obligation—to the extent that they are able to understand—to keep the lines of communication clear between themselves and their parents.

The Word says, "Obey your parents *in the Lord*" (Eph. 6:1). Paul is evidently speaking of Christian families where the obedience of the children to the parents would not violate Christian principles. Where does that leave children who do not have Christian parents? What are they to do? Are they free to ignore this command of God?

85

First of all, children should honor and respect their parents for *who* they are, even if they can't respect them for *what* they are. They are their parents. The young person who is trying to live a right life in the sight of the Lord is sometimes in a dilemma when faced with an order from an ungodly parent that goes against Christian practice. What is he or she to do? Where does his or her first allegiance lie? Is it to God or to the ungodly parent?

Although Ephesians says the commandment to obey one's parents "is the first commandment with a promise" (6:2), if we go back to Exodus, we find that there is also a "promise" with the second commandment: "You shall not make for yourself an idol in the form of anything in heaven above or on the earth beneath or in the waters below. You shall not bow down to them or worship them; for I, the Lord your God, am a jealous God, punishing the children for the sin of the fathers to the third and fourth generation of those who hate me, but showing love to thousands who love me and keep my commandments" (Exod. 20: 4-6). There should be no conflict here in the wording of the Ephesian passage, since it probably is dealing with children regarding their relationship with their parents. Paul is talking about families and their intertwined responsibilities, children's responsibilities toward their parents and parents' responsibilities toward their children.

Back to the ever important question of whom we should obey if there's a conflict. Through the Word of God we are told very plainly that our first accountability is to God Almighty, and we are first of all amenable to Him. This simply means that in all of life's dealings we are accountable to our Maker.

A drunken father or mother might order a son or daughter to do something that is morally wrong, something not right in the sight of God. And since the promise connected with this commandment is that we may enjoy from God a long and prosperous life, we cannot go against the other commandments in order to obey commands of profane parents. This, however, does not get the children "off the hook," since we have been talking about the extreme rather than the normal situation.

"Listen, my sons, to a father's instruction; pay attention and gain understanding" (Prov. 4:1). The reason for listening is to acquire, and profit by, understanding. Who could be a better teacher than the parent who has your best interest at heart and has been down the same road you are now traveling?

"But my parents want to run my life, pick my friends, and choose the places I go." Does that sound familiar? Often parents may act a bit overprotective, but if the parent really loves you, he or she is keenly interested in your friends and where you go. How about bringing your friends home with you and introducing them to your parents? People are usually afraid of those things they know little about, and even parents feel this way when it has to do with their children's friends. If they are nice, respectable friends there should be no reason for you not to want your parents to meet them. A little consideration on the part of the young man or lady in the home toward the parents goes a long way in promoting congenial communications.

Sometimes parental love goes beyond what is noticed by others. A small boy was asked in school, "How would you divide five pieces of pie at home between your mother, father, and four children?" He said, without hesitation, "That's easy, Mother would say, 'I don't want any pie, you fellows can have it all!'" Whether that little guy knew the extent of his mother's love or not, he knew that when there was a shortage, she did without so the rest of the family could have some.

Being the father of four daughters, I know very definitely about the matter of the fashion scene. Sometimes we just can't see the attractiveness of what "everybody else is wearing." Why does it have to be the latest in designer jeans, the most expensive shoes (that usually don't last as long as other, less expensive ones), and blouses with certain labels? I guess fathers are too often concerned with the cost or how they look rather than with what "everybody else is wearing." Please be patient with him, maybe he'll catch up before the style changes. Or maybe the style will catch up with him. I used to chide my dad for wearing those real wide ties that looked like aprons, because narrow ties were "in." A few years later I was wearing the same wide ties, since they were once again "newfangled" neckwear. The point is, respect your parents' opinions and wishes in the realm of fashion. *Your* respect will wear better than the latest fashions.

What about music? I consider myself a connoisseur of good music and I have tried to give my daughters, sometimes with very little success, an appreciation of the finer refinements of the art. But I have heard coming from their rooms some of the weirdest sounds being passed off as music. You see, I always felt that it took more than two or three notes or chords to make up a good piece of music. I still do feel this way, but I have decided that others have tastes too, and I suppose that if they can stand it, without injury to their ears, I can, for their sake, tolerate it.

There is one thing to be careful of in the area of music. The devil has his beat too. And hard rock has the devil's beat. It has been proven that the beat in hard rock causes young people to do things they would not otherwise do. Don't get "hooked" on hard rock. There is also music that is being called "Jesus rock." Be wary of that too. Let's keep sacred things sacred. Sometimes older folks are right, so don't discount *all* of their advice.

"Trust in the Lord with all your heart and lean not on your own understanding; in all your ways acknowledge him and he will make your paths straight" (Prov. 3:5-6). We all need guidance. If we lean too much on our own understanding, I'm afraid the props might be knocked out from under us. The Word goes on to say, "Do not be wise in your own eyes; fear the Lord and shun evil" (Prov. 3:7). Even if something *appears* evil, stay away from it! My mother gave me some good advice that I'll pass on to you. If you wouldn't want Jesus to find you doing something or being somewhere, it is a pretty good sign that you shouldn't do it or go there. I'll never forget that godly advice; I hope you won't either.

Some of the current songs have as their theme, do what you want to do because you're only young once; grab all you can while you're here. The problem with this kind of mentality is that you might grab the wrong thing and get more than you bargained for. The Bible says, "Remember your Creator in the days of your youth, before the days of trouble come and the years approach when you will say, 'I find no pleasure in them'" (Eccles. 12:1). The day *will* come when all those things that are so important in youth are no longer so important. Don't do anything while you're young that will hinder your service to God when you are older.

I've known many people who in their teen years forgot about their Creator and did things that "everyone was doing." These same people in their later years paid a high price for their careless living. Some had the indelible marks in their body of harmful habits acquired while they were young, marks that shortened their lives. Many of them found peace with their Creator in later years, but they paid a high price of forgetting Him in the days of their youth.

I've known women who, when they were young, did not follow their Creator and all through their adult lives were faced with the constant reminder of a child born without a father. The price of forgetting God in your youth is higher than any of you want or can afford to pay!

A wise parent realizes he or she doesn't know it all, and a wise young person realizes his or her parents do know more than he or she does. The parent was once the same age you are today and has already faced many of the tests you have to face every day; learn from their experience. You don't have to experience *everything* to be wise—you *can* learn from the experiences of others!

Concerning drugs, I offer simple advice—*don't try them!* Some would say, "I have to try them at least once to know what they're all about." That's exactly what the *devil* wants you to believe! There has been enough research, enough examples of what they do to you, and enough true stories of those who have tried drugs for you to understand that they only bring you *down*. Drugs will never be your friend and neither will alcohol!

Several years ago in Jacksonville, Florida, there was a billboard that pictured a drunk in the gutter, too drunk to get up. The caption read, "This is the finished product of the brewer's art!" Take it from me, I have seen enough results of drugs and alcohol within the state prison system to know the effect on the individual, on the family, and on the society in which we live; and it's all bad! My father said to me many times, "Son, don't take that first drink, and you'll never be an alcoholic." That's good advice for you to take too.

Some young people are passive or nonresistant when it comes to parental guidance, but many rebel at least on occasion. I guess it's not natural to swallow everything you're told, especially while you're a teenager. But the Bible says, "Children, obey your parents" (Col. 3:20). Obedience is the opposite of rebellion, and God is against the son or daughter who fights his or her parents. If you can't follow some directions while you're young, how do you expect to follow directions when you get out in the world where there is always somebody to tell you what to do? I once knew a girl who said of her mother, "Sometimes I'd like to kill her; it wouldn't bother me a bit!" If that young lady does not change her attitude toward authority, she has a rough life ahead of her and so does everyone who is associated with her.

It's so much better to learn respect for authority in a warm, loving setting in the home than later on with authorities who don't even care about you or your feelings. I've known some who never learned respect for those in authority until they learned it looking between bars. Thank God those are in the minority. Remember, a parent who, in the Lord, is correcting or instructing his or her son or daughter is doing it according to a divine mandate.

Some parents are continually "run over" by their children. I've seen parents who constantly take verbal as well as physical abuse from their offspring. I am certainly against child abuse, but I'm not too keen on parent abuse either. A parent is going against God's will when he or she allows this to happen without taking proper action. "Discipline your son, for in that there is hope; do not be a willing party to his death" (Prov. 19:18). The Word indicates that a son without discipline is headed toward a premature death. Don't be a willing party to it!

A son or daughter in the home should, when they reach an age of responsibility, have a voice in some of the affairs of the home as they relate to them. The good parent should follow the Golden Rule in rearing children. Treat them as you would want them to treat you if the shoe were on the other foot. I've known parents who treat their children in a very harsh manner because that's the way they were brought up. Let's be careful to give guidance, correction, and instruction according to what the Lord says rather than to try to get even with the unjust or unfair parents we may have had.

Bernard Shaw once said, "Youth is so wonderful, it's a shame to waste it on young people." Youth *is* wonderful, so use it wisely. Take advice from wise, caring parents. It is so good to leave your parents with good memories of *your* childhood.

Always be honest and fair with your parents; they

should be your best friends. It's good when sons and daughters can confide in their parents. I don't know at what age that is supposed to stop, if ever. I still confide in mine—the reason is that they are still my friends—they still care about their "boy." I've also noticed that the older I get, the smarter my father seems to get! Mark Twain once said, "I guess it's mainly because I finally came to realize he was pretty-well right most of the time."

The words "I love you" will go a long way with Mom and Dad. Show them your love every day, but saying it once in a while will help too. Even after you're grown and away from home, a love note to them will really make their day. And it's alright to show your affection toward them from time to time in public. You'll never know the thrill I get when, in public, one of my daughters gives me a little "peck" on the cheek or on top of the head.

According to the Bible your guidance and advice should come from *your parents,* not from the kids on the corner. It is not to say that you don't have friends, close friends at school or at church; but for the weighty matters of your life you should receive counsel from your *best* friends, your parents.

You won't always agree with your parents; you won't always want them to go with you and your friends; you will learn that they do not know all there is to know about everything. But you must always "honor your father and mother . . . that it may go well with you and that you may enjoy long life on the earth" (Eph. 6:2-3).

chapter eight

My hurt
really hurts

A young woman was walking away from the grave where her father's body lay. She collapsed in the arms of friends, who tried to comfort her in the best way they knew how, but it wasn't enough. The minister had read the Word of God that said, "Do not let your hearts be troubled. Trust in God; trust also in me" (Jn. 14:1). He had prayed, using the Scripture, "Praise be to the God and Father of our Lord Jesus Christ, the Father of compassion and the God of all comfort, who comforts us in all our troubles" (2 Cor. 1:3-4); yet she was not feeling that comfort as her knees buckled beneath her.

There are hurts in life that need more than the aspirin-bandaid approach. There are some wounds that go deeper than anyone on earth knows. Well-meaning friends attempt to give comfort with oft-used platitudes, such as "You'll feel better in the morning"; "I'll be praying for you"; and "In time the pain will lessen." But even with their best efforts, they all leave you hurting and crying and feeling like your world has just crashed!

The Bible says, "Cast all your anxiety on him because he cares for you" (1 Pet. 5:7). That is so easy, you might say, for the one who is not in the midst of the trial, heartache, or other disparaging situation to recite that truth to you; but look closely at the *whole* statement: "Because He cares for you!" That's what makes the difference! It is true that your friends care about you, but not in the same way He does! They can't care as deeply, and they are so limited in their well-intended consolation. But more than this, there is very little they *can do* about it. The same God who cares is the One who knows what you are feeling in your deepest disappointments and darkest dismay. He knows because He's been there!

The Son of God came in the Person of Jesus, taking on human flesh. John quotes Him as saying, "I and the Father are one" (Jn. 10:30). This same Jesus tasted the sufferings of all mankind, so that God the Father might know, through Him, just how you feel! "Because he himself suffered when he was tempted, he is able to help those who are being tempted" (Heb. 2:18).

"No temptation has seized you except what is common to man. And God is faithful; he will not let you be tempted beyond what you can bear. But when you are tempted, he will also provide a way out so that you can stand up under it" (1 Cor. 10:13). Just think! He knows; He cares; He understands; and He will not let more come your way than you can handle! He is the Author of *victory*! Victory over whatever your hurt is!

Do you remember how Jesus was tempted, tested, tried, and saddened? Matthew, along with Mark and Luke, tells that He was ". . . led by the Spirit into the desert to be tempted by the devil" (4:1). After forty days of fasting, "the tempter came to him and said, 'If you are the Son of God, tell these stones to become bread'" (4:3). He was tested through a very human drive, that of physical hunger. When this was rejected, the devil then tested Him through the powers that He already possessed and tempted Him to exploit God's miraculous might. Finally the author of temptation, ". . . took him to a very high mountain and showed him all the kingdoms of the world and their splendor. 'All this I will give you,' he said, 'if you will bow down and worship me'" (4:8-9). He was tempted to obtain authority through ungodly means as the devil flashed a panoramic view of the entire world before Him. He was promised all those things that the devil might promise you and me in our times of testing, but Jesus said, "Away from me, Satan!" (4:10), and "angels came and attended him" (4:11). What an exciting revelation! God, through Jesus, went through all I'll ever have to contend with and is able to show compassion for me and my needs.

"For we do not have a high priest who is unable to sympathize with our weaknesses, but we have one who has been tempted in every way, just as we are—yet was without sin" (Heb. 4:15). Whatever your problem—He can understand and sympathize. Too often we try to work things out on our own and fail to avail ourselves of all the resources of heaven through Jesus. "Let us then approach the throne of grace with confidence, so that we may receive mercy and find grace to help us in our time of need" (Heb. 4:16). My friend, you can stand on that truth! It's God's promise to *you*!

Thousands of individuals all over the world are hurting for a variety of reasons. Some have been let down by their friends; others feel lonely and forsaken; some are worn nearly to the limit by sickness. Some have financial problems and reverses that seem unsolvable; others have decisions to make that will affect the rest of their lives. Many for whom He died are suffering silently with the misery known only to themselves and God.

Let's look at the verse that probably depicts the grieving human best of all: "Jesus wept" (Jn. 11:35). This verse that portrays the sorrowing Jesus may be the shortest one in the Bible, but it ranks as one of the most meaningful in terms of human value! The human, caring, feeling Jesus cried! He is the same One who hears me when I cry!

The same Jesus who looked at His disciples through disappointed eyes, clouded with tears when they deserted Him, looks on my disappointments. He knows how it feels to be rejected, hurt, forsaken, have hopes dashed, suffer injustice, and even lose a loved one through death. He even tasted abandonment in the hour of death: "My God, why have you forsaken me?" (Mt. 27:46). It's no wonder the Word tells us that He experienced everything we'll ever run up against in our lifetime.

The Scriptures tell us that He even went "a little farther" (Mt. 26:39) than we'll ever have to go. Although forsaken by

His father at His time of death, God promised in Deuteronomy 31:6 and then reaffirmed it in Hebrews 13:5, "Never will I leave you; never will I forsake you."

Oh yes, Jesus went farther in this matter of hurting than we'll ever have to go. He suffered more for more things than we'll ever have to endure. He was rejected by more people than will ever reject us. He had less of the goods of this world than we'll ever have.

Often in times of acute anguish, there is only a moment for a short, "Lord help me!" But with Jesus on the listening end of that desperate plea, help is on the way. I believe that the Lord has angels just waiting for a summons from Him so that they might wing their way to the aid of one of His troubled children.

The Psalmist assures us in God's Word that God "will command his angels concerning you to guard you in all your ways" (Ps. 91:11). Read the entire ninety-first Psalm. When God's people call, help is on the way! The late Dr. V. Raymond Edman, in his book, *The Disciplines of Life,* says, "In the Christian life there are hours of distresses, discouragement, darkness and danger. There are also moments of despair, intense, exacting, excruciating; moments when life and death are in the balance, and we have no strength nor wisdom to top the balance in our favor. We cannot strive nor struggle, flee nor even faint; we can only cry unto God. . . . If He hears us not, and helps us not instantaneously, all is lost. Helpless is the heart that in that brief instant knows not to whom it can cry; on the contrary, happy is the heart, however harrowing may be the experience, that knows Him whose ear is not heavy that He cannot hear nor His arm shortened that He cannot save."[1]

I received a call late one night and the anguished voice blurted out, "My boy's been shot!" The details were still incomplete but that grief-stricken mother in the surgical waiting room only knew that her teen-age son was in surgery and possibly would not survive. I arrived at the hospital a few minutes later to find her and the rest of the family wringing their hands as they waited in that smoke-filled little room. Throughout the night we waited, prayed, and read the Word of God together until finally, after many tense hours, the doctors came to tell her that her son was out of surgery but not yet out of trouble since there was a great danger of fatal infection from the wound.

She had called on the Lord before, but this was the most serious thing that had ever happened in her life. And God did not fail her: for as we had read the Word and prayed throughout the surgery, she got a calm assurance from the Lord that whatever happened, He was going to be with her. He had promised to be her refuge and fortress, her God, in whom she could trust (see Ps. 91:2).

I like to personalize the Bible to my own needs. I think that's what God intended when He had it preserved through the ages for us. I believe God intends all the promises to be *mine personally.* "Jim will call upon me, and I will answer him; I will be with Jim in trouble, I will deliver Jim and honor him" (see Ps. 91:15). There was a little song we used

[1] Dr. V. Raymond Edman, *The Disciplines of Life* (Reprinted by Harvest House Publishers, 1982), p. 121.

to sing when I was a boy; its message still holds true today as it did then:

Every promise in the Book is mine,
Every chapter, every verse, every line

"The Lord knows those who are his" (2 Tim. 2:19). It's so important in times of need to realize for certain that you are His. You know and God knows. There are some times when the problem is so immediate or so pressing that there is no time to really pray about the matter. A man who was very sick told me that he had at times been in such pain that he could not have prayed if he had to. I've experienced the same kind of urgency.

There are other situations not quite as urgent, but painful just the same. There are often hurts surrounding our work situations. Some people seem to forge ahead on the job, and the promotions all come their way, while you get your job done very efficiently, are sincere about your work, and get better results than the other workers. But since you don't "polish the apple" and assert yourself to those who give out the advancements, you do not get as much as a hint of appreciation or promotion. You just fret under it all.

But Jesus is the great Equalizer! He will eventually set the records straight! When? The Word often says that God did what He did "at the proper time." In God's time, at the *best* time, when *He* was ready, when the time was right. "Let us not become weary in doing good, for at the proper time we will reap a harvest if we do not give up. Therefore, as we have opportunity, let us do good to all people" (Gal. 6:9-10).

The Bible says here, do good, keep your attitude right, don't give up doing what is right, and God will reward you according to His time schedule. God probably has a better promotion waiting for you than the one you had your heart set on.

As our daughters have grown old enough, they have found after-school jobs. We have always stressed the fact that Sunday is the Lord's day, and we don't do unnecessary labor on that day. On every job they have cleared this with the boss *before* they took the position, and God has always honored their faithfulness to Him in this matter.

Daughter number three once got a job with the same company that her two older sisters had worked for years before. The agreement was reached about Sunday work, and everything was understood that she could not work that day. She would work at other times and relieve some of those who did work on Sunday, but that's all. One Saturday the boss came to her saying, "Tomorrow you'll have to work." She reminded him of their agreement, to which he replied, "Everybody works tomorrow, it's the company anniversary, and if you don't come in tomorrow just don't come in on Monday after school either." When she came home we talked about the situation realizing that it was out of her hands now and in God's. The next day we all went to church and she didn't go to work. You guessed it, Monday when she went in the boss sent her home.

No job. No money. We prayed about it, and I said,

"Honey, God has a better job for you than you had anyway." Within two weeks she had a job that was far better with more money, more benefits, Thanksgiving and Christmas bonuses, vacation pay, profit sharing, and every holiday off with pay. Not bad for a high school student! She kept that job until she got married and moved out of the city.

Does God answer prayer when there is a hurt like this? Absolutely! "We will reap a harvest if we do not give up" (Gal. 6:9b).

Hurts come in assorted ways and with varying degrees of pain, but they're hurts just the same. A trusted friend betrays your confidence—you hurt! (Remember, Jesus knew what it was to have a friend betray His confidence and He hurt too. Judas even betrayed under the pretense of being one of His best friends—with a kiss.)

A wife of many years leaves her husband with only a note left for him to find when he comes home from work. He's been faithful to her and provided for the two children and her needs. Now she's gone! The note indicates that she left with another man. The hurt is now even more unbearably painful; to leave is bad enough, but with another man! This husband hurts and hurts deeply!

Does Jesus care when my heart is pained
Too deeply for mirth and song,
As the burdens press, and the cares distress,
And the way grows weary and long?

Oh yes, He cares; I know He cares.
His heart is touched with my grief.

> *When the days are weary, the long nights dreary,*
> *I know my Savior cares.*[2]

"Does Jesus Care?", Frank E. Gracff

An ex-husband tries to turn a child away from its mother. He seeks to defame her good name to the child and to the community. Although she and her friends know that the things he is alleging are all false, she still hurts. She would like to confront him and his friends in a way that there would be no more accusations. She'd really like to get even. "Do not be deceived: God cannot be mocked! A man reaps what he sows. The one who sows to please his sinful nature, from that nature will reap destruction; the one who sows to please the Spirit, from the Spirit will reap eternal life" (Gal. 6:7-8).

The Bible says that God will get even for you and you won't need to do a thing except continue to "do good to all people" (Gal. 6:10).

A preacher was once told by a parishioner that the place the congregation had picked out for him to reside was "good enough for him" and that "beggars can't be choosers." He and his wife both hurt! The hurt is quickened when they think of the very elegant home so impressively furnished in which that parishioner lives. Oh yes, preachers are people too, and they are sometimes hurt. Does God care? In Psalm 20 God reminds us "that the Lord saves his anointed; he answers him from his holy heaven with the saving power of his right hand" (v. 6).

[2] Frank E. Gracff/J. Lincoln Hall, "Does Jesus Care?" (Kansas City, Mo.: Lillenas Publishing Co.). © 1959 by Lillenas Publishing Co. All rights reserved. Used by permission.

Sometimes when you feel that you've "had it up to here," remember that the Word tells us in 1 Corinthians, chapter 13, that love is the greatest. Love is the strongest weapon with which the Christian has to fight injustice. There is a popular song that has in its words, "Nothing cures like time and love." Give God time and you exercise love—He'll right every wrong and straighten out every crooked deal you've had come your way.

Often hurts come from those within the church who are supposed to be on the same side as you. The devil has a way of taking words and turning them around, thus the hearer gets quite a different message than was intended by the speaker. The Word says, "God is not the author of confusion, but of peace, as in all churches of the saints" (1 Cor. 14:33 KJV). When a hurt comes through a member of your church, remember where it comes from—not from God. I am not about to excuse everything people in the church do and say. There are those who delight in keeping things stirred up. There are some that take offense at anything that is said. I'll just let the Lord, whose body it is, take care of them.

I've known some in one church who had trouble with almost everyone, so they went to another church. Alas! They had trouble there too, so they moved to another church, but trouble seemed to follow them. I think of the saying that goes, If you have trouble with your neighbor and you move, and you have trouble with your neighbor and you move, and you have trouble with your neighbor—it's not the neighbor.

When these hurts come, don't succumb to them but use them to mount higher as you overcome. The Bible says, "In all these things we are more than conquerors through him who loved us" (Rom. 8:37). That's through Jesus! We can overcome through Jesus rather than come under. Read on. Paul says, "For I am convinced that neither death nor life, neither angels nor demons, neither the present nor the future, nor any power, neither height nor depth, nor anything else in all creation, will be able to separate us from the love of God that is in Christ Jesus our Lord" (Rom. 8:38-39). Now it's time to *praise the Lord*!

Many elderly people are also hurting. Never think that just because you have overcome your youth and young adult years that it's smooth sailing from then on. Sometimes the worst hurts come to those who are in what we term "the golden years."

Jake was eighty-four years old, was never married, and had no family except a distant cousin somewhere. He lived next door to us, and we tried to befriend him when we learned that he had nobody at all who cared. We tried to show him we cared. We invited him to dinner on his eighty-fourth birthday, the same day the United States was 200 years old. He said, "I'll have to keep a lookout for my friends from the country club; they're going to have a big celebration for me tonight." We ate and kept an eye out for his country club friends. They never came. He went home later, and they still didn't show up. All day he waited, dressed up, looking for them. Jake was forgotten! He had plenty of "friends" while he was able to get around and be a part of the social activities with his "friends" and spend his money on them, which at one time he had a lot of. But now he was too old and feeble—and he was soon forgotten. Jake died all alone.

No family, no friends except those who knew him just a short time next door and tried to befriend him.

It's sad, but there are thousands in the same situation. Some have families who have forsaken them and only contact them when they want a handout. They sit day after day in their loneliness and with their disappointments.

In Saint Petersburg there was an old man who lived next to my wife's parents. They would take him food and occasionally he would go to church with them. When he was physically able he would go down to the pier and sit on a bench and talk to whoever came along. Several summers he had written home and told his family that he was making plans to come back home for the summer, but the reply was always, "Dad, you're doing all right down there, and we all have our own families to look after; you'd better just stay there." For years that old, sick, disappointed, lonely man sat in his one-room apartment. He had a lot of money, but his family had it tied up and doled out just enough for him to live on in his little "prison."

Jesus loves little children, but he loves big children too! "I will do whatever you ask in my name, so that the Son may bring glory to the Father. You may ask me anything in my name, and I will do it" (Jn. 14:13-14). What do you need? Ask God in Jesus' name, and receive! Is your hurt beyond description; does no one else know how it feels? Ask God for help. God's Word promises help for those who are hurting; His word cannot fail. "Heaven and earth will pass away, but my words will never pass away" (Mt. 24:35; Mk. 13:31; Lk. 21:33).

An old man used to stand in church to testify and say that his favorite Scripture was "and it came to pass." His explanation was that when problems came; when sadness surrounded him; when unexplained troubles, loneliness, and all the other hurts of life flooded him, the Word of God says in several places, "It came *to pass.*" It didn't come *to stay*! Jesus would see to it that it would pass!

When you hurt, let your troubled heart walk with Jesus through the Bible.

appendix

Problems and Bible solutions

Problem	What the Bible Advises
The boss at my job is constantly critical.	Josh. 24:14-15; Ps. 37:1-40; Mt. 5:9, 11-16, 23-24, 43-48; 11:28-30; 12:33-37; 1 Cor. 10:13; 2 Cor. 12:7-10; Phil. 4:4-9; Col. 3:12-14; 4:6; 1 Tim. 2:1-2; Heb. 12:14-15; Jas. 1:2-8, 12; 3:1-12; 5:7-12
If I change jobs, I might fail.	2 Ki. 17:1-16; Ps. 37:25; Mt. 6:5-13, 19-21, 25-34; Lk. 12:22-31; 2 Cor. 9:6-11
Yesterday my husband was fired.	Josh. 24:14-15; 1 Ki. 17:1-16; Ps. 37:25; Mt. 6:5-13, 25-34; 11:28-30; Lk. 10:38-42; 12:22-31; 2 Cor. 9:6-11; Phil. 4:4-9; Jas. 1:2-8, 12; 5:7-12

Problem	What the Bible Advises
Our elderly parents live too far away for visits.	Ps. 37:25; 71:17-18; Mt. 19:4-6; Phil. 4:4-9; Jas. 5:7-12, 13-20
My brother or my wife's brother is an alcoholic.	Ps. 9:10; 22:11-15, 19, 22, 24; Mt. 7:7-11; 11:28-30; 20:29-34; Mk. 11:22-24; Lk. 11:1-10; 15:25-32; 1 Cor. 13; Col. 3:12-14; Heb. 2:18; 11
I can't stop smoking.	Josh. 24:14-15; Ps. 9:10; 18:6-19; 22:11-15, 19, 22, 24; Mt. 7:7-11; 11:28-30; 20:29-34; Mk. 11:22-24; Lk. 11:1-10; 1 Cor. 10:13; Heb. 2:18; 4:14-16; Jas. 1:5-8; 4:7-10
My oldest child constantly talks back to me.	Exod. 20:12; Deut. 4:9-10; Josh. 24:14-15; Prov. 13:1-3, 24; 15:1-2; 19:18; 22:6, 15; 23:13-14, 22; Eccles. 12:1; Eph. 6:1-4; Heb. 12:5-11; Jas. 3:1-14
My children refuse to attend Sunday school.	Deut. 4:9-10; 6:4-7; Josh. 24:14-15; Prov. 13:1-3, 13-17; 19:18; 22:6; 23:22; Eccles. 12:1; Acts 10:1-4; 16:29-34; Eph. 6:1-4; 2 Tim. 3:14-17; Heb. 10:19-25; 12:5-11
My parents ignore and avoid their grandchildren.	Josh. 24:14-15; Prov. 15:1-2; 17:6; Mt. 5:9, 23-24; 11:28-30; 1 Cor. 13; 2 Cor. 12:7-10;

Problem	What the Bible Advises
	Phil. 4:4-9; Col. 3:12-14; Titus 2:1-5; Heb. 12:14-15; Jas. 1:2-8, 12; 3:1-12; 5:7-12
My wife makes more money than I do.	Prov. 6:34; 31:10-31; Mt. 6:19-21; Eph. 5:21:33; 1 Pet. 3:7
My husband wants to relocate and I don't.	Gen. 2:7, 18-25; Mt. 5:9; 6:5-13; 19:4-6; Lk. 10:38-42; 12:22-31; Eph. 5:21-33; Col. 3:18-21; Heb. 12:14-15; 1 Pet. 3:1-6
My doctor told me my baby is retarded.	Josh. 24:14-15; Ps. 37:3-8; 127:3-5; Mt. 6:5-13; 2 Cor. 9:8; 12:7-10; Phil. 4:4-9; Heb. 2:18; Jas. 1:2-8, 12-13; 5:7-18
Someone accused my son of thievery.	Exod. 20:15; Deut. 6:4-7; Josh. 24:14-15; Prov. 13:1-3, 24; 19:18; 22:6; 23:13-14, 22; Eccles. 12:1; Mt. 11:28-31 Gal. 6:1-8; Eph. 4:25-29; 6:1-4; Heb. 12:5-11
My daughter refuses to help around the house.	Deut. 6:4-7; Josh. 24:14-15; Prov. 13:24; 19:18; 22:6, 15; 23:22; Eccles. 12:1; Lk.10:38-42; Heb. 12:5-11
I can't get a job.	Josh. 24:14-15; 1 Ki. 17:1-16; Mt. 6:5-13, 25-34; Lk. 10:38-42; 12:22-31; 2 Cor. 9:6-11; Phil. 4:4-9; Jas. 5:7-13

I realize this list by no means covers every question that plagues us in our daily living; nor is the list of Bible references complete. But they do give a starting point that will hopefully lead the reader to a more careful study of the Bible and give him or her a deeper appreciation for the solutions the Bible offers to problems of daily living.

Bibliography

Dobson, James, *Dare to Discipline*. Wheaton, Ill.: Tyndale House Publishers, 1970.

Edman, V. Raymond, *The Disciplines of Life*. Minneapolis, Minn.: World Wide Publications, 1948.

Gracff, Frank E., *Does Jesus Care?* Kansas City, Mo.: Lillenas Publishing Co.

Hamilton, James D., *Directions*. Kansas City, Mo.: Beacon Hill Press, 1976.

Harper, A.F., *The Story of Ourselves*. Kansas City, Mo.: Beacon Hill Press, 1962.

Hendricks, Howard G., *Say It with Love*. Wheaton, Ill.: Victor Books, 1972.

The Holy Bible, New International Version (NIV), copyrighted 1978 by the New York International Bible Society.

Knight, Walter B., *Knight's Master Book of New Illustrations,* Grand Rapids, Mi.: Wm. B. Eerdmans Publishing Company, 1956.

Petersen, J. Allen (ed.), *The Marriage Affair,* Wheaton, Ill.: Tyndale House Publishers, 1971.

Mumford, Bob, *Living Happily Ever After.* Old Tappan, N.J.: Fleming H. Revell Company, 1973.

New American Standard Bible (NASB), The Lockman Foundation, 1960.

Riley, John E., *This Holy Estate,* Kansas City, Mo.: Beacon Hill Press, 1957.